TRENCH TEACHING

Proven Tactics for the High School Teacher

Learn how to control the balance of power in your classroom!

By Phillip Schreiber

With Daniel Fisher

TRENCH TEACHING

Dedicated to
Linda Whiting and Griz E Bear

TRENCH TEACHING: Proven Tactics for the High School Teacher
Copyright © 2002 by The Trench Teaching Consortium

Requests for information should be addressed to:

THE TRENCH TEACHING CONSORTIUM
PO Box 215, Owings, MD 20736

Visit the TRENCH TEACHING Website at www.trenchteaching.com

Library of Congress Cataloging-in-Publication Data

Schreiber, Phillip.

   Trench Teaching: Proven Tactics for the High School Teacher

   ISBN 0-9720710-0-8

   Library of Congress Control Number: 2002105659

Designed and produced by PrintComm Partners, Inc.
www.printcomm.ws

Printed and bound in the United States of America

Contents

TRENCH TEACHING

The goal of teachers in the trenches is to reestablish classroom control and mutual respect through a return of student responsibility and discipline, while building a bridge from adolescence to adulthood.

The Icons

Throughout the text you'll find icons that call your attention to important nuggets of truth or neat things to ponder or hints for success that you may not have considered. Each one is a special bit of information that you will need to know at some time or another.

The Authors

Phil Schreiber, "TEACH" himself, has 30 years' experience teaching (8 years at the junior high and 22 years at the high school level). Phil, who specializes in working with the unmotivated and academically challenged, is uniquely qualified to deal with these students because he was once a so-called problem student. With hard work and perseverance, Phil turned his life around and began a long path of achievement including a B.S. from the University of Maryland, two masters' degrees (M.A., M.S.) and an administrative certification. He's also served as coordinator for the local American-Japanese Student Exchange and promoted more than 12 Black Belts as Director of a Karate School and Co-Director of a National Training Camp. He's also an accomplished writer, penning numerous editorials in local and national newspapers.

Dan Fisher was an accomplished teacher for 7 years, and then left due to burnout. He became a journalist for a year at a local newspaper and has since returned to the profession he missed and loves. His remarkable experience offers insight into staying fresh, motivated and efficient as a teacher. In fact, he shares how to draw boundaries between home and work so you can go the distance in this rewarding profession. By the way, Dan received his B.A. and M.A. from the University of Maryland.

Foreword

There are probably two questions you are asking yourself about this book: "What am I going to get out of it?" and "Who are these guys?"

Glad you asked. Unlike most other books in this field, this book is written FOR high school teachers BY high school teachers ... not "K through anything" ... not middle school, not college. High school.

What Am I Going to Get Out of It?

We have three goals:

1. To reduce your stress in the classroom, thereby making your daily life easier.

2. To teach you how to deal with the 10% of your students who make you a success or failure as a teacher.

3. To help you survive your 30-year tour of duty and end up happy and financially secure.

We'll discuss classroom management, grading, referrals and even give you useful words and phrases for parent interactions. These ideas can easily put you in a win-win position with administrators, parents and students. To help you approach daily problems, we'll use lots of anecdotes from our personal experiences to illustrate ways to handle even the most difficult student and situation.

Why Should We Listen to These Guys?

Well, I [Phil] was one of those troubled students you read about, or who maybe sits in the back of your classroom today. I was that slow reader who had bad grades, a lackadaisical attitude, couldn't stay on task. To make matters worse, my father died when I was 13, so my mother had to go to work. There wasn't any help from the school about how to study or how to get better grades. There wasn't even a government program to help me! I remember wanting to do well, but I didn't have a clue how one would ever go about getting an A or B.

A few key people were instrumental in encouraging me as a youth. While I was participating in rugby and karate, they taught me to keep going after I'd been hit, to be responsible to my teammates and to achieve personal goals of physical and mental discipline. These were the keys to success!

Once I possessed these keys, the real struggle began ... I had to catch up. I had to make up for all the time I had wasted in my early years before I had any desire to learn. Looking back, I only wish I had had a teacher in high school like the teacher I later became. In spite of everything, I managed to graduate from high school and go to college.

Why did I become a teacher? I have often asked myself that question in various frames of mind. All I can say is that I looked up to teachers when I was a student. A teacher was a person who conveyed wisdom and knowledge. A passing of the baton, so to speak. I saw weaknesses in some teachers and felt I could do better.

I saw teaching as an opportunity to alter deviant behavior, such as the things I did that plagued me during my early educational years. It was a chance to give back some of what I had learned through different experiences.

Remember, many general level students are bright but have low levels of maturity and personal direction. Your job is to help them cross over the bridge to adulthood. I've been described by a high-ranking state education official as "part intimidator" and "part humanist." You may have to become this strange breed as well, while you push your students (sometimes kicking and screaming, figuratively speaking!) toward that bridge.

The greatest gifts you can pass on to your students are not just the academics but also the desire and the methodology for success. Show them HOW to get that A, and say good-bye to discipline problems. These gifts will stay with them long after your academics have been forgotten.

Teaching is a multi-layered profession, ranging from academics to compassion, embodying a sense of humor and toughness. It means staying focused and loyal to your beliefs within an educational world that is often confusing and sometimes threatening. During your upcoming teaching journey, **EXPECT** satisfaction and financial rewards while overcoming educational obstacles and prejudices.

1: Getting Hired

A necessary evil in securing a teaching job is filling out the application. When completing this dry document of personal information, remember that someone else will be scrutinizing it. The people in the personnel department look for individuals who possess many talents and abilities. The application should include outside interests that demonstrate your ability to handle extracurricular activities. These extra aptitudes will be crucial during your first few years in a school.

When submitting a résumé, make it accurate, simple, short and to the point. Do not be shy concerning your accomplishments. Design it to show that you're a person whose past demonstrates potential future achievement. An old friend of mine who was a principal once told me that **the best way to succeed in an interview is to control it.** How? By submitting your résumé in an easy-to-read outline form. Why? Because usually all members of the review or interviewing board will have a copy of your résumé, and most of their questions will be generated from the material they have in front of them. The format should resemble something like this:

NAME
Address
Telephone Number

Career Objective
Work Experience
Education
Extra Information
Reference with Telephone Number

Remember the "screener" for a position will only spend a minute or two reading this document.

Make your application reach out and grab the reader.

You should have a cover letter, keeping in mind the following:

- Don't exceed one page in length.
- Clearly indicate the position for which you are applying.
- Be concise.
- Don't be modest.

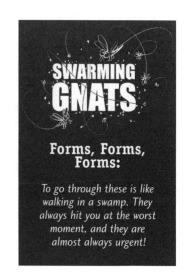

SWARMING GNATS

Forms, Forms, Forms:

To go through these is like walking in a swamp. They always hit you at the worst moment, and they are almost always urgent!

Once you've submitted your typed application, sit back and wait for a call from a secretary indicating the time and place of your upcoming interview. If you don't hear within a reasonable amount of time (7-10 days), call to ask about the status of your application. Never assume anything!

The Interview

Congratulations! You've secured an interview. Be sure to verify the time and date. Also, ask for the names and titles of the interviewers and say how much you look forward to meeting them. During the interval between the filing of your application and the actual interview, it is very smart to practice your responses to the possible questions. Also, you should research the school system and local points of interest before your interview.

You will be greeted by the receptionist as the review board sharpens their knives and forks in anticipation of the main course ... you.

Before you arrive at the school district's central office, be ready for action, and dress conservatively. Remember, the world of education is also the world of big business; act accordingly. You will be greeted by the receptionist as the review board sharpens their knives and forks in anticipation of the main course ... you. During your wait time, remember everything you can about the local school district area, the types of questions you will be asked and what questions you will ask.

Once you take your seat before the interviewers, everyone will be all smiles and anxious to have a go at you, as they size you up during the preliminaries. Your primary advantage is they need you to fill a position.

Just remember what they are looking for: a multifaceted person who can work with two or three clubs and more than one academic discipline.

Also, they're observing your personality. Do you exude confidence in your knowledge and ability to handle classroom problems? You might need to give yourself a pep talk before the interview if you lack confidence.

During the interview, be yourself. Warm interaction is key to making a good first impression. Allow the panel to control the process. Interview time is limited. They may evaluate you with a 1- to 10-point system. **The secret is to match your philosophy with theirs**—without compromising your own values, of course. In addition think about the following during this interview process:

- Look directly at the interviewer who asks you the question. Eye contact is very important.

- Be conscious of how you speak and what words you use.

- Be honest. Do not try to cover up something that you're unsure of.

Furthermore, be ready for some type of written response to a question after the first interview. You will probably be asked to write about your philosophy of education. This is to ensure that you have control of the English language and grammar.

Below is a list of questions a high school principal put at the top of his list while interviewing a candidate:

1. Describe a daily lesson from beginning to end.

2. Describe your grading philosophy.

3. Are you willing to help with extracurricular activities?

4. Describe the resources you would use to improve non-motivated and/or discipline concerns in your classroom.

5. Discuss two of your strengths as a teacher and two of your weaknesses.

6. In your opinion what is the key component to teaching a class?

7. Where do you see yourself in 5 years?

8. The last indicator is not a question, but a gut feeling of how he or she will fit our staff chemistry based on their demeanor and how he or she answered the questions.

In short, be prepared to stay on your toes. A long time ago, I went for an interview for a teaching job and the interviewer asked me, "Can I call your previous principal for a recommendation?" After some thought I said, "You can call, but you will not get a good recommendation." I explained what had happened. I then sat patiently waiting for the hammer to fall. His response was, "Thank you, Mr. S., for being honest. I've been in this business a long time and, when I was younger, I was in a similar situation. If you're still interested, we would like to have you on the staff." The point is that many of your interviewers know BS when they hear it and do appreciate truthfulness!

The Bottom Line:

1. Research the school system ahead of time.
2. Have specific details in mind about lessons and grading.
3. Have questions ready to ask during the interview.
4. Extracurricular interests make you an attractive hire.
5. Be confident.
6. Be as natural as possible. Don't try too hard.

2: You're Hired! Now What?

Soon, all too soon, a hundred or more students will enter your classroom. Some look forward to getting back to school. But for many, it looks like a drag after having a few months off. Think back to when you were in high school ... fingers often crossed that school would be canceled, or at least delayed, with every flurry of snow.

Of course, preparation is on your mind before school starts. You've probably just come out of a program that required you to show your lesson plans for approval, or at least constructive criticism. I had a professor require a typed 14-page lesson plan. The absurdity of adding minute-by-minute response times and "expected responses" made the plan feel like a science experiment to be performed on unsuspecting teenagers. **Teaching is not a quantifiable scientific endeavor; it's a living organism comprised of a teacher and students.** So there are two components to preparation: the conceptual and the practical.

The conceptual—how you frame what learning and teaching are—must come first. If you don't have a clear sense, a strong sense, of what a successful classroom looks like, take the time to get it clear in your mind. Without this conceptual foundation, the practical lesson planning aspects of the job will become an absurd conglomeration of school exercises, only things to check off a massive required curriculum list.

Some key components of the foundation include interaction, interaction, interaction ... not a stack of worksheets (called "dittos" in the olden days!) to fill in with umpteen blank spaces, "busy work." If you must use them, use them sparingly and only to improve classroom management if you have trouble keeping students focused. Most students resent heavy ditto work.

Picture yourself in a classroom as a student. We've all been there. What teachers scored high marks with you? Draw on that experience. You may even want to write down your favorite three teachers and list reasons why they made your list. Then think back to the teachers who created classrooms you couldn't wait to leave. Why? It may sound corny, but write down their names and what you can remember about those horrible experiences to create a concrete image in your mind.

You'll need to hold onto these images, particularly as the frenetic pace of the school year begins and you start to forget why you bothered to try teaching in the first place.

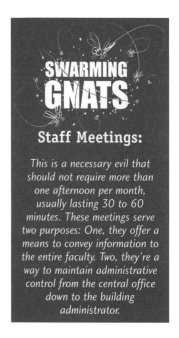

SWARMING GNATS

Staff Meetings:

This is a necessary evil that should not require more than one afternoon per month, usually lasting 30 to 60 minutes. These meetings serve two purposes: One, they offer a means to convey information to the entire faculty. Two, they're a way to maintain administrative control from the central office down to the building administrator.

So, once you have this clear picture in your mind—what a good teacher is and what a successful classroom looks like—it's time to get down to the nuts and bolts of preparation.

You'll probably have a curriculum, a stack of textbooks (including teachers' editions) and a school handbook chock full of information.

- Don't sweat the handbook unless you want to overwhelm yourself with minutia. It has little to do with teaching—only with procedures, policies and parking assignments. Read it once. Don't try to memorize it. Within a few months you'll discover what is really necessary from the handbook. Don't lose it. It's a must at staff meetings.

- Look over the curriculum for essential categories. To avoid being overwhelmed by a bulky binder of information, it's helpful to distill the essentials down to one page if possible.

At the beginning of the school year, I leaf through the binder while jotting notes on a piece of looseleaf. When I'm finished, I tack that page up next to my desk or somewhere within easy reach. It will serve as a guide throughout the year.

For English there will probably be a novel unit, drama unit, short story unit and poetry unit. You may want to make a list of the required novels, plays, short stories and poems. After you teach the required works, check them off; this will ensure you haven't missed anything when the final exam rolls around.

Ask another teacher if the final exams are standardized in your county. If they are, your curriculum essentials checklist will be invaluable as the year progresses. If questions appear about *The Red Pony* by John Steinbeck and you didn't have time to teach it, or you just plain forgot about it, the students will lose those exam points. As for you, well, test accountability is on the rise, and official eyes are on your students' scores. **Help the students score well and you'll score well, too.**

For English classes I also list the papers the students are required to write. Chances are the students will have to write a research paper, a personal essay and at least one essay analyzing a literary text. **Avoid assigning all the essays within a quarter unless you want to drown in your own red ink.**

As a beginning teacher, it's crucial to have a sense of what you are required to teach. You will then become a good teacher and increase your chances of attaining tenure.

Speaking of tenure, most people are greatly misinformed about it. It simply means "due process." A teacher with tenure cannot be dismissed without this process according to local statutes and state laws. Normally it will take a minimum of 2 years of observations and negotiations to force a teacher from a position.

If a person does not have tenure, then there is no formal process. You could be asked to leave at the end of any teaching year if you don't have the security of tenure. Your departure, however, must still conform to local statutes.

As a new teacher, set your sights on tenure. Once you have it, you may want to take more risks with creative lessons that may not "fit" your administrator's idea of strong teaching.

Always make sure you can justify how each lesson is related, directly or indirectly, to the official curriculum. If you're creative this is not difficult. Just have it thought out in your mind ahead of time.

Some teachers like to plan months in advance, day by day. That's ridiculous. That makes school a formula: "Plug in teacher. Plug in students. Hit ON switch." In reality, some lessons will stretch out over time. Some will die even before hatching.

A good lesson will always consist of a warmup, body and conclusion.

- Make a rough map of what you want to cover the first quarter. You want to have room to flex within the parameters you set up for yourself. You may want to list what you are required to cover and then create a list of the most logical order in which to knock out the material.

- Estimating the time it may take to cover each item isn't a bad idea. Just don't lock yourself into a rigid plan, unless creating a classroom of cogs is your thing. Keep it living and dynamic. If something excites you one week, an idea hits you, run with it before it fades. Jump out of the prepackaged blah blah blah. The students will enjoy the class more and so will you. And more learning will be going on, too.

… during the first year, it's okay to cling to the curriculum and the required textbooks as life rafts.

- It's a good idea to skim the required textbooks. Just don't box yourself in. During the first year, however, it's okay to cling to the curriculum and the required textbooks as life rafts.
- And don't forget to talk to an experienced teacher. He or she will be an invaluable resource throughout the year concerning all aspects of the school and school district.

The Bottom Line:

1. Design lessons that facilitate interaction with students.
2. Have a clear sense of the attributes of an excellent teacher.
3. Have a sense of where you're going a few months in advance but stay flexible.
4. If you're bored, the students will be too.
5. Skim required textbooks but don't get suffocated by them.
6. Supplement text with present-day examples.
7. Think of lessons that will give your students many opportunities to succeed.
8. Always have a "Plan B" in mind if your lesson begins to stall.

3: First-Day Preparations

After winning the job, it would be a good idea to spend some time in your new building prior to the required reporting date. This will allow you some private time with your new principal, administrators and librarian. Also, it will give you the extra time you will need to prepare your room and to get comfortable with your new situation. You might consider the following actions in your new room:

1. Organize the student desks and set up areas for isolation.

2. Position your desk for supervision.

3. Decorate the walls.

4. Position the computer and other audiovisual aids.

5. Locate the needed room supplies.

Decorating the classroom before students arrive is important. First impressions really stick. Make your room a place full of stimulating visuals, but don't overwhelm them with wall-to-wall lists and charts of information. Keep a balance in the room. If you don't like this aspect of teaching, call a friend to help you out. Also, remember that most people are right-handed. As a result they usually look to the right first. Keep this simple fact in mind when setting up your room.

Your personal appearance counts just like the appearance of the room. So, look professional and act accordingly. During your first year, many people will be sizing you up. Be aware!

Seating charts are helpful both for learning the students' names and for classroom management. You'll get your class lists before school starts. Fill in the seating chart with names from the list. On that first day, get the students in seats where you can call on them by name. The students will see you're in charge and taking the job seriously.

TEACH SEZ:

Learning their names quickly is important to create a strong classroom. The students will respect you for it; they'll see you care. Once you learn all their names, which is really the reason for creating a seating chart in the first place, use discretion regarding new seating arrangements. For my well-behaved students, I often toss the seating

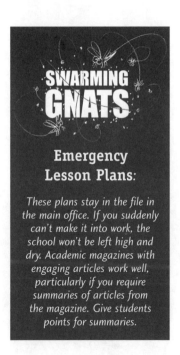

chart in the trash after I learn their names. For unruly students, the seating chart may function as a key classroom management tool, shifting students away from talkative friends.

On the first day, have the students fill out 3x5 index cards for your file. Name, address, phone number and parents' names should be written on the cards. You may need to make a phone call home after the first day! In the beginning, organization is particularly crucial to your classroom. Establishing rules, assigning lockers, issuing books and distributing administrative handouts take up the first week.

Classroom rules are a good idea. Just don't make too many. A few basics like "Be on time," "Be prepared" and "Raise your hand to speak" may be useful at the beginning of the school year. Some classes may even need "Do not leave your seat without permission." Some teachers type a letter of expectations to be read and signed by the student and the student's parent. And returned, of course. These may come in handy at a parent conference later.

So, to summarize: Get a clear picture in your mind of what good teaching looks like. Read/skim through the materials. List what you've got to cover and estimate how long it will take to do. Stay flexible with lesson planning. Decorate a bit. Make a few clear classroom rules, not more than three or four. And it doesn't hurt to explain your rationale for the decisions you make. Many students will respond better if they know why you do what you do.

Lastly teaching consists of three parts:

1. **Conveyance of the curriculum.**
2. **Instruction of a study methodology.**
3. **Training for adulthood.**

The Bottom Line:

1. Use a seating chart. (Some teachers switch them each quarter to diminish cliques.)
2. Learn names quickly.
3. Make a few classroom rules.
4. Create a visually attractive learning environment.
5. Develop a fluid mindset about teaching.
6. During your first year, you must learn school procedures, the curriculum, student names and, finally, concentrate on student behaviors. Trust me, it will get easier next year!

Opening Day Checklist

THINGS TO DO	Periods	1	2	3	4	5	6
Index Address Cards		✔	✔	✔	✔	✔	✔
Seating Chart		✔		✔			
Issuing Books		✔	✔	✔			
Assigning Lockers		✔					
Fire Drill Information		✔		✔			
Tardiness Procedure		✔					
Grading Procedure		✔		✔			
Personal Expectations		✔	✔				
Classroom Rules		✔		✔		✔	
Point Sheet		✔			✔		✔

By adapting this method, it will help you stay organized through the first week. It will be very easy to forget what you have said and what you might have forgotten to say. Use my checklist to create your own.

Sample Teacher Opening Day Remarks

"It's always to your advantage to see my good side."

"You choose what happens to you in this room."

"As far as I'm concerned, this year represents a new piece of paper— what goes on it is up to you!"

"Make your decision NOW: Choose the A or choose the F. It's your decision."

"Get away from the idea of liking and not liking; just decide to do it!"

"Report to class just like your parents or guardians would report to the job."

"If you want nice things to happen to you, then decide what you need to do to make it so!"

"Please copy down the information off the board for the first page of your notes."

Here are two icebreakers that I often use, "Survival in the Desert" and "Lost on the Moon." These Opening Day games are great vehicles for getting your students to think and strategize while they're getting to know you and their classmates.

SURVIVAL IN THE DESERT*

It is approximately 10:00 a.m. in mid July and you have just crash-landed in the Sonora Desert in southwestern United States. The light twin-engine plane, containing the bodies of the pilot and the co-pilot, has completely burned. Only the airframe remains. None of the rest of you has been injured.

The pilot was unable to notify anyone of your position before the crash. However, ground sightings, taken before you crashed, indicated that you are 65 miles off the course that was filed in your VFR Flight Plan. The pilot had indicated before you crashed that you were approximately 70 miles south-southwest of a mining camp which is the nearest known habitation.

The immediate area is quite flat and, except for an occasional barrel and saguaros cacti, appears to be rather barren. The last weather report indicated that temperatures would reach 110°—which means that the temperature within a foot of the surface will hit 130°. You are dressed in lightweight clothing—short-sleeved shirts, pants, socks and street shoes. Everyone has a handkerchief. Collectively your pockets contain $2.83 in change, $85 in bills, a pack of cigarettes and a ballpoint pen.

THE PROBLEM

Before the plane caught fire, your group was able to salvage the 15 items listed below. Your task is to rank these items according to their importance for your survival, starting with "1" (the most important) to "15" (the least important).

You may assume that the number of survivors is the same as the number on your team and the team has agreed to stick together.

Step 1: Each member of the team is to rank each item as they individually perceive its importance. Do not discuss the situation or problem until each member has finished the individual ranking. Once discussion begins, do not change your individual ranking.

Step 2: After everyone has finished, as a team rank the 15 items in order of importance.

Individual Rankings:
___ .45 Caliber Pistol (loaded)
___ Book: *Edible Animals of the Desert*
___ Bottle of Salt Tablets (1000)
___ 1 Quart of Water per Person
___ Red and White Parachute
___ Compress Kit with Gauze
___ 2 Quarts of 180 Proof Vodka
___ Sectional Air Map for Area
___ Flashlight
___ Jack knife
___ 1 Topcoat per Person
___ Plastic Raincoat
___ Two Pairs of Sunglasses
___ Cosmetic Mirror
___ Magnetic Compass

Team Rankings:
___ .45 Caliber Pistol (loaded)
___ Book: *Edible Animals of the Desert*
___ Bottle of Salt Tablets (1000)
___ 1 Quart of Water per Person
___ Red and White Parachute
___ Compress Kit with Gauze
___ 2 Quarts of 180 Proof Vodka
___ Sectional Air Map for Area
___ Flashlight
___ Jack knife
___ 1 Topcoat per Person
___ Plastic Raincoat
___ Two Pairs of Sunglasses
___ Cosmetic Mirror
___ Magnetic Compass

*Spencer Kagan: Cooperative Learning Resources for Teachers

SURVIVAL EXPERT'S RANKING*

Source: Air Force Survival Training Manual

First and foremost, you should decide to stay at the crash site.

1   **Cosmetic Mirror**—In the sun, the mirror can produce bright light and be seen for several miles.

2   **1 Topcoat per Person**—Best thing to do is attempt to restrict the airflow around your body to decrease the amount of water evaporation that results in dehydration and death.

3   **1 Quart of Water per Person**—Will keep you "comfortable" for a while.

4   **Flashlight**—Helpful to aid searches after dusk. Also, with batteries removed, the case can be used as a container for the plastic still described below.

5   **Red and White Parachute**—To produce shade by spreading parachute over the airframe of the plane.

6   **Jack knife**—Because cactus is available, you can use the knife to cut the cactus and use it in a homemade still to obtain moisture from the barrel and saguaros cacti.

7   **Plastic Raincoat**—Knife and raincoat go together to develop plastic still.

8   **.45 Caliber Pistol (loaded)**—Dangerous item to have because of physical and emotional stress of the group.

9   **Two Pair of Sunglasses**

10   **Compress Kit with Gauze**—Not needed because no one is injured and you should not be leaving the crash site.

11   **Magnetic Compass**—Not needed because you should not attempt to walk from the crash site.

12   **Sectional Air Map for Area**—Not needed because you should not attempt to walk from the crash site.

13   **Book: *Edible Animals of the Desert***—Should not expend your energy attempting to leave the crash site to hunt.

14   **2 Quarts of 180 Proof Vodka**—Little value since the effect of alcohol on your system is to draw water in order to absorb the alcohol into your system.

15   **Bottle of Salt Tablets (1000)**—Will actually rob your body of moisture.

*Spencer Kagan: Cooperative Learning Resources for Teachers

LOST ON THE MOON

You are in a space crew originally scheduled to rendezvous with a mothership on the lighted surface of the moon. Mechanical difficulties, however, have forced your ship to crash land at a spot some 200 miles from the rendezvous point. The rough landing damaged much of the equipment aboard. Because survival depends on reaching the mothership, the most critical items available must be chosen for the 200-mile trip. The 15 items left intact after landing are listed below. Your task is to rank them in terms of their importance to the crew in its attempt to reach the rendezvous point. Place a 1 by the most important item, 2 by the second most important, and so on through the least important, 15.

___ Box of Matches

___ Food Concentrates

___ 50 Feet of Nylon Rope

___ Parachute Silk

___ Portable Heating Unit

___ Two .45 Caliber Pistols

___ One Case Dehydrated Milk

___ Two 100-Pound Tanks of Oxygen

___ Stellar Map of the Moon's Constellations

___ Life Raft Containing CO_2 Bottles

___ Magnetic Compass

___ 5 Gallons of Water

___ Signal Flares

___ First-Aid Kit Containing Injection Needles

___ Solar-Powered FM Receiver-Transmitter

FM radio, my foot! I can't even find an "oldies" station!

LOST ON THE MOON RANKINGS

Below are the correct rankings for the items, as determined by the Space-Survival Unit of NASA:

15 Box of Matches (little or no use on the moon)

4 Food Concentrate (supply daily food required)

6 50 Feet of Rope (useful in tying injured, help in climbing)

8 Parachute Silk (shelter against sun's rays)

13 Portable Heating Unit (useful only if party landed on dark side)

11 Two .45 Caliber Pistols (self-propulsion devices could be made from them)

12 One Case Dehydrated Milk (food, mixes with water for drinking)

1 Two 100-Pound Tanks of Oxygen (fills respiration requirement)

3 Stellar Map of the Moon's Constellation (one of the principal means for finding directions)

9 Life Raft (CO_2 bottles for self-propulsion across chasms)

14 Magnetic Compass (probably no magnetized poles, thus useless)

2 Five Gallons of Water (replenishes loss by sweating, etc.)

10 Signal Flares (distress call within line of sight)

7 First Aid Kit Containing Injection Needles (oral pills or injection medicine valuable)

5 Solar Powered FM Receiver-Transmitter (distress signal transmitter, possible communication with mothership).

What do I do now?
Add water and stir?

4: The Daily Routine

What happens after I get through the first day? The daily grind. **Always allow yourself at least 10 to 15 minutes in the morning to organize your day and get mentally ready.** It takes an enormous amount of energy to teach 5 days a week ... week in and week out!

Get sleep. Take vitamins. Exercise.

Structuring your week often puts students at ease. Vocabulary quizzes on Wednesdays and tests on Fridays, for example, help students feel less overwhelmed. **The key to the daily routine is to find variety within structure.**

A routine that has worked well for me has been "Movie Clip Monday" – "Topic Talk Tuesday" – "Wordskills Wednesday" – "Three Thoughts Thursday" – and "Freewriting Friday." These activities take from 10 to 15 minutes to complete and provide anchors to each lesson planning day.

On **Movie Clip Monday**, we watch a 5- to 10-minute film clip, which provides an excellent springboard for fun and interesting writing prompts. Pick clips you like and pick a variety. The ones I've shown include claymation, a chase scene, music video, parody of *Star Wars* and Robin Williams giving a poetry lesson in *Dead Poet's Society.* My students have written poems, descriptive paragraphs and identified the theme or message of the film clips, depending on the clip. They really enjoy this, and it's a great way to start off the week.

On **Topic Talk Tuesday**, usually during the last 10 to 12 minutes of class, students write two topics on a small piece of paper they tear out of their notebooks. These scraps are collected and put in a hat. When I call on a student, he or she draws a paper and speaks to the class for 15 seconds. Topics can range from "old socks" to "broccoli" to "facial hair." The students get a kick out of hearing someone pick their topic. As the year progresses, increase the time to 30 or 45 seconds. After the student finishes speaking, he or she chooses the next speaker. The object is to make students more comfortable talking in front of a group. By the end of the year, even the shy students enjoy the exercise.

On **Wordskills Wednesday** the class focuses on vocabulary. A friend of mine, Mike Jameson, gave me this idea ... which then triggered my thoughts for the other 4 days of the week. This day is self-explanatory: teach vocabulary and grammar, within textual context whenever possible.

On **Three Thoughts Thursday**, three questions are put on the board for students to answer as a warm-up. There may be current event issues,

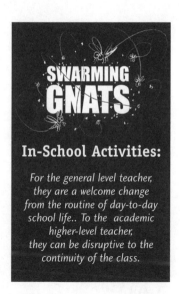

SWARMING GNATS

In-School Activities:

For the general level teacher, they are a welcome change from the routine of day-to-day school life.. To the academic higher-level teacher, they can be disruptive to the continuity of the class.

TEACH SEZ:

personal reflection questions and creative writing questions. "Should the United States kill Osama bin Laden if he's caught? Explain." "Write an extended metaphor for how you're feeling today." "Does absolute truth exist? Explain." You get the idea. Get them thinking and writing about a myriad of things. It's also intellectually healthy for students to make connections between different disciplines. You can help them with your variety of questions.

On **Freewriting Friday** students write for 8 minutes straight without stopping, often to music. They can write whatever they choose as long as they keep writing. This helps them develop new ideas, purge emotions and just plain enjoy writing. It's another way to engage youthful minds. **Do not read their freewriting; if you do, it will no longer be so free!** Students should be able to write one side of a page in the 8 minutes if they are writing continually.

Many schools require a warm-up activity to be on the board along with objectives for the day's lesson. A warm-up is not supposed to be longer than about 10 minutes. This could simply be a question on the board to lead into the day's lesson. Examples include, "What do you think makes a short story interesting to read?" or "What does the word moral mean to you?" The warm-up can also serve as a review, forming a bridge between yesterday's and today's lessons, i.e., "List the eight parts of speech" or "Describe three of the story's characters."

Of course, if the warm-up leads to a great discussion, it's generally productive in the long run to go with it. **Some administrators may applaud "going with it," while others want a stricter, more legalistic approach. Know your administrator!**

Every lesson should have a list of objectives clearly written on the board. An example might be: "Student Will Be Able To" **[SWBAT]**

- Identify figures of speech in poetry.

- Create extended metaphors.

- Write an effective introductory paragraph for an essay.

Try to develop lesson plans and activities that take from 2 to 3 days to execute. Or use a film every 7 to 10 days to give yourself a chance to correct papers. After showing a film, a useful activity might be for students to write a summary of their opinions, using good sentence structure and grammar.

Create variety to keep yourself and the students from being lulled to sleep. One day, a debate; the next, a hands-on activity. Then add a

SWBAT

- **IDENTIFY FIGURES OF SPEECH IN POETRY**
- **CREATE EXTENDED METAPHORS**
- **WRITE AN EFFECTIVE INTRODUCTORY PARAGRAPH FOR AN ESSAY**

game or two. Film clips are also handy for discussion starters. Showing a movie doesn't necessarily mean the whole period. Find a pertinent, stimulating clip (5 to 10 minutes long) and springboard off it. You may find that your students remember the visual, engaging clip long after the class is ended. Try to have an alternative method ready for students who might have difficulty grasping your primary methodology.

Lecturing is the least effective way to teach. Students recall about 5 percent of material taught through lecture. Think back to lectures you sat through and how much your mind wandered. Engage your students with discussion and group work. Be ready to repeat and reinforce your message. Advertisers sometimes plan to present their message up to nine times to a consumer. A real perk in the teaching profession is this:

FOOD FOR THOUGHT

> **If you're bored with your own class, you have the power to change it.**

You may want to ask students for feedback at the end of each quarter. Their input matters and may give you a better sense of when you're hitting the mark and when you're missing.

Weekends are downtime 90% of the time! You'll probably find that weekends will be your personal catch-up time. Always allow yourself ample weekend time to enjoy whatever you wish. The weekend can also be a good time to get a mental picture of what the week ahead will look like—probably a balance of quizzes, homework assignments and a test, perhaps. Our goal is for you to work smartly and efficiently, so that you will be able to relax as much as possible during your off hours and thus avoid burnout.

Remember, you must learn to budget your time and efforts, using school time as much as possible, just like marathon runners budget their energy. This is not a sprint but a long 30-year race to the finish!

Once you engage in the battle of learning, it will be a battle that is continuous, lasting the duration of the school year and perhaps into the summer and following year. Never back off. Your students must adjust to you. Be unyielding in your war against their natural tendency toward excusism. It will be the one of the best gifts anyone could ever give them!

Daily Procedures:

1. Keep a file of daily Attendance Bulletins.
2. Use 10-15 minutes every morning to prioritize your upcoming day.
3. Always check for students who are AWOL from your class.
4. Take attendance during your warm-up session.
5. During 1st period, always record the code number of a student's absence.
6. Use your school time as efficiently as possible.
7. Keep a record of meetings and appointments on a monthly calendar.
8. Confront behavioral problems during the months of September and October.
9. Keep a record of negative student behaviors and actions in your gradebook. Use dots in the gradebook (see page 56 for example).
10. Remember, YOU begin and dismiss a class; not the bell.
11. Always be ready to alter your seating chart if problems develop.
12. Save energy; pick your battles.

The Bottom Line:

1. Get sleep.
2. Exercise.
3. Use film clips, games, any resources available.
4. Welcome student feedback.
5. Make war on excusism.
6. Whenever possible use the weekend to relax.
7. Always have Mondays well prepared before you leave on Friday. That's the only way to enjoy Sundays!

Once you engage in the battle of learning, it will be a battle that is continuous ... Be unyielding in your war against their natural tendency toward excusism. It will be one of the best gifts anyone could ever give them!

5: Who Are These Kids?

Take a moment and think back to when you sat in a high school classroom surrounded by your friends and supporters. Think about your thoughts then and perhaps even your youthful drives and dreams. In many cases, what was important to you does not interest the majority of students today. Yes, of course, some things never change; but the entire mode of thinking is different today.

This difference is caused primarily by mass communication, MTV and the internet. Many students simply never have the chance to enjoy a prolonged childhood anymore before being forced into adulthood armed only with an adolescent mentality. This creates a situation where many students falsely feel that they are on an equal level and have the same privileges as their teachers and other adults. They are totally unaware that these privileges should be earned over decades of living.

Also, many have been taught or have assumed that the easy way is the best way to get the prize. As a result, their work ethic may be weak. **Sacrifice that leads to reward is a concept that has never existed for many of them.**

With this in mind, teachers must realize that many students are simply the end result of the society in which they live. They are, to a degree, victims of circumstance. How can I assert this? Let's take a look at their surroundings. Our culture promotes and embraces the concepts of victimization, self-indulgence, entitlement, "excusism," shamelessness and multimillion-dollar sports contracts as normal. Traditional home values have been replaced by finance companies and their instantaneous gratification; kids have been taught that feelings are more important than accomplishment and competence. These students often lack self-discipline, self-accountability and self-control, thinking instead that "standards" are dictated by the lowest common denominator!

This is where you can help them greatly!

I remember one time when I denied a student his request to leave the classroom. "How can you say that?" he asked. I calmly stated, "Watch my lips. No." Some of these kids have never been confronted with the concepts of denial and failure—concepts that often surface aggressively when grades are assigned.

For example, I had a nice student who was concerned about his grade. I said, "Be sure to get your assignments completed by the deadline next

week so you can earn a good grade." He responded by saying, "You know I'm really trying! Can I still get an A?" Here's the true story. This young man was missing 15 out of 20 assignments and had been sleeping in class off and on for more than a week. How could the idea of an A even enter his mind? Most students do not know what reality really is.

Students sometimes lose track of how they're doing in your class. A child with a 30% average in your class may approach you with a confused look after report cards are distributed. "How did this happen?" **As the teacher, you should consider giving monthly updates of grades to help students stay on track.** But that's your call.

Another thing to remember is something that always fascinated me about the relationship between classwork and the students. The percentage of As and Fs seldom changes, whether I make the class easy or difficult. Some students choose to do their work; some don't. It's an attitude thing.

When I was a karate student many years ago, I attended class three times a week for 3 years, even though I knew the material. There were no shortcuts. It was always the same: repetition, repetition, repetition! The end result was a total person with a grasp of knowledge, maturity and physical skills. Concepts of learning in the Far East contrast sharply with our culture. The bottom line: shortcuts aren't part of the Eastern mindset.

Take the above situation and compare to today's secondary school. The emphasis shifted long ago from repetition and basics to fun, fantasy and feeling good. New teachers must attempt to bridge this gap. **Remember, learning how to learn is hard work, but it can still be an enjoyable process and journey.** If properly taught, learning is a skill that will follow your students for the remainder of their lives—not just the academic information but having the skill to know how to learn and process information beyond the classroom.

...teachers must realize that many students are simply the end result of the society in which they live. They are, to a degree, victims of circumstance.

Selective Hearing

It's time to elaborate on specific problems you may encounter in the classroom. The major reasons for student failure in school are weak listening skills, immaturity and a "so what" mindset (also called "bad attitude").

Some students have refined "selective hearing" to an art form. This underlies their failure to do well. In their minds, what you have to say is secondary to what they are talking or thinking about. Using their frame of reference, only the moment and the events of the upcoming weekend are important. Watch how their listening skills change when you begin to discuss the weekend.

Poor listening skills become quite obvious when you give instructions to the class. Even though you may repeat the instructions of the day, inevitably a number of students will ask, "What page or what drawing am I supposed to do?" To them, it is the teacher's inability to teach or instruct, not their inattention, that creates the difficulty. Some don't have a clue what they're doing wrong. My response is usually, "I'm sorry. I already said that three times; please get it from one of your friends."

Other examples of poor listening skills include the following: If I say, "Don't turn in any new class work until Monday!" there will always be about 20 percent who still turn in the new work. I might say, "I will collect your notebooks at the end of class." Again, at least 20 percent will come and ask me, "When should I turn in my notebook?"

No matter what directive you give, be prepared for at least 20 percent to snap on their selective listening caps, asking you to repeat your instructions later.

The Excuse Game

Students often have difficulty understanding responsibility. When a child comes to class late or without a textbook, he or she makes excuses. Perhaps it's the human condition, though some say it's the adolescent condition. They might believe that because schools are responsible institutions, they do not have to be responsible individuals!

"It's not my fault!" a student may say. Because it wasn't the class's fault or the teacher's, the blame should be attached to the student in question. Here is a challenge for you: get a student to say, "OOPS, my fault—sorry about that," and with a minimal penalty.

I remember one time I had to proctor a history exam during "Finals Week." After trying for a while to get the students to settle down and be quiet, I began to hand out the exam booklets and the "Scantron" answer sheets. When I completed my task, I looked up and saw a number of students with their hands up to ask a question. Now, what do you think their questions were? Believe it or not, "May I borrow a pencil?" Knowing that this test would be corrected by a computer, they had come to their final exam totally unprepared. But in their minds, it was my fault for not having enough pencils, rather than accepting their own lack of preparation and responsibility.

Many students' concept of a deadline is the night after the work is due. I remember one student, after being out sick 3 consecutive days, saying, "I need 3 additional days to complete the work!" I said, "No. You've had 4 weeks to complete the work; all work is still due tomorrow, except for yesterday's assignment." She was not very happy and complained to the front office. They said it was up to me. Next case!

If a child has a genuine learning disability and needs more time to finish work, you will learn this from his individual educational program (given to you by a person from the Special Education Department) or from the child's parent. **Remember, you're working with people; so be humane, fair and consistent at all times.** If a child truly has a problem, be prepared to modify your operational procedure. It's no big deal!

Displaced responsibility often shows up in the learning process itself. Many students feel that just attending class is good enough to pass— without any understanding of their role in the learning process and the work requirements.

How do you treat students who do not care or make any attempt at all to complete the curriculum?

Simple, make their classroom lives so uncomfortable that they will be willing to do almost anything to get you off their backs. Believe me, it works. For many students this attitude change is the beginning of their road to success.

As an example, treat the hardworking students as adults and the non-working students as elementary children. This difference will be seen and understood. Most kids do not want to be on your bad side. When you begin to hear, "That's not fair," your plan is beginning to take hold! My response to that statement would be, "You're absolutely correct. Very good. Now, what are you going to do to change this situation?" Remember, the purpose of this is to get them to change to you, not you change to them!

Children often have a distorted sense of what is real and what is fantasy. More than a few high school students think a Lexus and a $100,000 salary are easily within reach, say in the next few years. I happened to overhear a few students talking one day about a possible job as a specialty chef. "$150,000 ain't no problem!" This ignorance, along with the idea that everything must be fun, contributes to student misconceptions of the real world.

It is easier for many of them to grasp the concept of fantasy (top grades without work, success without struggle and failure, and a future without hardships) than to make the connection between today's efforts and tomorrow's success.

Because we live in a world of instant communication and fast food, almost all students have a difficult time with the idea of patience, learning and maturation. I find that many of them, when confronted with a task, choose not to complete it because they do not see instant results. This can best be seen in their shortcut approach to long-range problems.

EXAMPLE ASSIGNMENT

10 one-page summaries of articles with each article attached.

Deadline: 8 weeks

When I give the above assignment, I can expect to receive anything from zero effort to the completed assignment. Getting students to perform at a 60% level can sometimes be like pulling teeth. Motivated kids probably represent about 25% of the high school population. But even these kids have problems with long-term goals and hard work.

When I was young, I spent a lot of time on the rugby field and in karate classes. I was greatly impressed by the courage of the contestants. I made many friends during those activities, including a man 20 years older than myself (sort of a surrogate father). One day I told him my thoughts on the concept of courage (playing and fighting), and to this day I remember his response. "Phily, the real courage is to get up every day year after year and go to work!"

Now that I'm middle-aged, I fully understand the meaning of his comment. I've watched many of my friends struggle to hold down long-term jobs. How does this relate to what we're talking about? The students of today are similar to my old friends in that they constantly need overwhelming levels of stimuli in order to get through the day. Who will be there to get the students up at 6 a.m. to go to work everyday to support a family? If they cannot learn to set goals and motivate themselves now, they will have difficulty later on. Remember, they will always choose the easy way and not necessarily the correct way unless taught differently.

"Phily, the real courage is to get up every day year after year and go to work!"

Why? Because it seems that many students lack a personal system of values and beliefs. The beliefs they do have are distorted by negative cultural influences. Observe the manner in which they dress to report to school, their speech and even their posture. They must be taught that reporting to the classroom is similar to reporting to the workplace as an adult. Even students who choose not to perform are probably still nice kids. They just haven't matured yet.

Guidance Pass:

A good rule to follow is to allow students to go the guidance department, until you are told differently. Remember to hold the students accountable for what they miss while out of your class.

90 percent of your students will be delightful. It's that other 10 percent that will keep you on your toes. Many of them come from dysfunctional homes. Many of them need strong parental role models. Deep down, most children really want to succeed. Don't let the negative events of a day or week overshadow the positive ones that have also occurred. I know that is so much easier said than done, but please work on it!

Common Student Responses

1. I don't care!
2. No way.
3. No!
4. Whatever!
5. Huhhhh!
6. What's for lunch?
7. May I go to the bathroom?
8. Ain't my fault!
9. I'll never do this in real life!
10. You're not my parent!
11. No big thing!
12. I wasn't doing _____!
13. Don't mean a thing!
14. I didn't do it!
15. Why?
16. What did you say?
17. I don't care.
18. Wait until my mother calls!
19. What are you talking about?

Sample Nonverbal Student Responses

1. Shaking of the head in disgust
2. Avoidance and passive-aggressive behavior ("Whatever!")
3. Loud talking and laughing when you are speaking
4. Not showing up for detention

It's almost impossible for me to tell you what counterstatements will be effective and which ones will not. The best rule to go by is to act within your personality. **Say things that are natural to you but not "directly" insulting to the students.**

Oh, I almost forgot, **do not even think about cursing**. This presents a fine line, because it is not wise to allow the student to gain momentum. You must be clever enough to use your wit without breaking the above rules. Please feel free to modify them for your own personality.

Teacher Verbal Responses

1. Since you don't care—move.

2. Choose to do it or choose not to ... your decision!

3. Get Out!

4. "Whatever" is an adolescent passive-aggressive way of avoiding reality. At this moment I'm your reality.

5. That's not the correct response.

6. I do not have a clue; now let's get back to work.

7. Of course you weren't—but—

8. I know where you're heading, because I've already been there.

9. Tell that story to someone else; please don't use it on me.

10. Excuse me, I already said that.

11. Fine, I look forward to speaking with your parents.

12. Don't ask me why! Just choose to do it or choose not to!

13. Don't shake your head at me!

14. I do not take abuse from adults, let alone adolescents!

15. Now that you've finished with your temper tantrum, let's try it all over again!

16. I don't understand why you want to fail and come back next year.

17. I've given you the chance to act like an adult. You've chosen to act like a 6th grader.

18. Remember, I want you to get an A. That's why I'm leaning on you. Understand?

19. What you're telling me by your actions is that you've finished the work and are ready for more! Is that true?

20. It's your choice. The consequences of your decision will be yours.

21. That is the incorrect response.

22. I am your teacher and legally you are my responsibility.

The Bottom Line:

1. Don't accept a shortcut mentality in your students. Hard work is the way.
2. Teach students about real consequences of behavior.
3. Don't let negative events engulf positive classroom experiences.
4. Maturity will come in time for your students. Be patient.
5. Be a role model.
6. Students will do what they are allowed to do.

6: Classroom Management

By far the most important aspect of any part of teaching is how you run your classroom. Everything centers on this simple concept. Or is it so simple? How do you want students to see you as the teacher? Do you want to be liked or respected? Some say, "Don't smile until Thanksgiving," fearful the students will run over a beginning teacher. To be liked by students doesn't mean you're their buddy. But let's face it, we all can remember teachers we both liked **and** respected.

Trying to explain classroom management is like trying to hold water in your hands. It's not easy. You must focus on control, firmness and respect. One of our well-respected colleagues refers to himself as a "benevolent dictator." The classroom will represent 90 percent of your professional life. It must be a place where you're in control.

The level of control you exercise in the classroom is directly proportional to the level of stress you'll experience during the day.

The tougher you are in September and October, the easier it will be for you from November to June. Remember, kids want limits and controls. It adds to their feeling of security and safety. Without firm, established limits and parameters, chaos will be your constant companion.

Everything you do should have a purpose. Remember, all eyes are on you. Students know the difference between BS and sincerity. Be direct. And above all else, learn to anticipate what's coming next: within a discussion, within an argument and within your lesson.

How students perceive you is crucial to your interaction with them. Be yourself! Be polite, positive and firm! Don't worry about being nice — that will happen naturally. Avoid sarcasm or belittling remarks; those will contribute to your own classroom demise. Everyone has favorites and dislikes; that's OK. Just don't act on them! Be consistent. **Any inconsistencies, accusations of favoritism and the like will quickly be noted by the students—usually aloud—and sometimes to the administration.** Students will respect you if you're consistent and firm. Yet there's room for mercy when special circumstances arise—such as a grandmother's death, car accident of a close friend or recovery from an illness. Sometimes a student may not feel well for whatever reason. As a result, it is important to be aware of this and cut the student some

FOOD FOR THOUGHT

slack! Don't forget to be human. It's okay for teachers to care. Students respect that. Studies have shown that people learn most from people they both respect and relate to.

You're there to teach. The students need to learn normalcy within the classroom setting and, from this microcosm, how society operates. But before any of that can happen, control has to be established, including discipline. The "D" word conjures up many visions, but in our minds it means students know their limits and the consequences when they exceed them. **Remember, your biggest enemies are not defiance and stupidity but ignorance and immaturity.**

As for waiting until Thanksgiving to smile, that advice is crazy. Good teachers clearly communicate they care—through preparation, consistency and enthusiasm. Have you ever seen an enthusiastic person who didn't smile?

Let your love for your subject matter show. Let your attitude be contagious! Your attitude will draw them in much more than trying not to smile. Furthermore, most students can see right through you when you're trying to be unnaturally tough. And if there's one thing young people will nail you on it's insincerity—which relates to hypocrisy— "putting on a mask."

Be yourself as much as possible. Teaching is both the most complex and simplest of professions. If you treat students with respect and set up clear parameters for class conduct, you will have a fruitful time together. As you look around your school, you quickly learn that the best teachers are both liked and respected. Weak teachers are simply liked, because students run those classes. And teachers just concerned about respect are usually resented as uptight curmudgeons who are only concerned about control.

Find ways to help students be successful and you will have fewer problems. It may be easier to control your class if students are succeeding. One way I help students in this area is to stand slightly behind a rowdy student or group of students and just watch them. This has an unnerving effect on them and also keeps them on task.

Respect is crucial—for themselves, for their peers and for you as the final authority. Of course, students will know you're new, no matter how much you try to shed that image. For every new teacher the greatest challenge is this issue of classroom management. Oh, if they're still behaving after the first few days, don't get too confident. They're simply sizing you up. At this point, they know the game better than you! After a month, you'll have a sense of how well you're actually managing the class.

One way I help students in this area is to stand slightly behind a rowdy student or group of students and just watch them. This has an unnerving effect on them and also keeps them on task.

You need a clear strategy before school begins on how to deal with student attitudes, levels of maturity and listening skills. Giving students responsibility for their own success and centering the class on a "point sheet" is often helpful, inviting them to participate in the evaluation process. I always find that making an analogy to employer-employee evaluations helps to establish the correct class atmosphere. It usually takes 3 to 6 weeks for them to fully understand. They need opportunities to make decisions and deal with the consequences, for better or for worse.

Mistakes are OK, as long as they learn from them. You will see many changes in your students from September to December, then another shift from January to May. Always have alternatives thought out in advance.

Your position as teacher must be respected. Students discuss teachers plenty outside class. It is always best to command respect; but, when all else fails, demand it! Establish your reputation early and pray it's a good one; for example, that you're someone who is kind, yet doesn't take any crap. Remember as a new teacher, you are establishing a reputation that will precede you in the years to come. So, be precise and deliberate in your actions and comments.

You are not their big buddy. Mentor, yes. Role model, yes. Partner in learning, yes! That is what they really want from you. Don't be fooled into discovering your second childhood. Again, do not try to become their buddy! If you do, you may as well kiss your career goodbye.

Do not tolerate rudeness or excusism. Do not tolerate passive-aggressive behavior: shaking of head or "whatever!" (Refer to list of teacher responses.) If students are still talking after you begin class, what do you do? Yell? Definitely not. You can stand there and wait, but that usually doesn't work—not to mention you're handing control over class time to them. Redirect their attention with an "Excuse me, class is starting now. We have important material to cover. You may choose to participate now or after school."

If they continue to talk, don't hesitate to write one of them up and send them out. Identify a leader, particularly a trouble-making leader. Sending that person out may go a long way to showing the class you're in charge. If necessary, hold the entire class after the dismissal bell to make up for the lost time in the beginning. They'll catch on. They'll see you're willing to take action. Many teachers threaten and then don't do anything. Do not get in that habit. If you threaten to do something, do it. Period.

Don't be fooled into discovering your second childhood. ... Do not try to become their buddy!

If you do, you may as well kiss your career goodbye.

For those of you with a background in the military, think back to those experiences. Think about the chain of command. You always knew who was in charge, where you stood and what would happen if you did not follow directives. It's exactly the same in teaching and working a classroom. Except here you are a platoon sergeant and a company commanding officer in one, with a chain of command above you. This doesn't mean you can't be polite.

Many students enjoy being treated like adults, hearing a Mr., Ms., or Sir when being addressed. It sets a tone for the class, like an adult going to the workplace. Remember that students will mess up and you must be able to handle their mistakes. Don't hold grudges against students. It's most important for them to learn that kindness begets kindness, but rudeness brings on severe consequences. **The golden rule is at the core here, "Do unto others as you would have them do unto you."**

Remember, sometimes requesting an administrator, teacher or student conference will work in lieu of giving a referral.

TEACH SEZ:

To succeed in class, a student must master both his emotional maturity and the academics. Without maturity in place, academics will be an uphill struggle. Start with a seating chart, as mentioned earlier in chapter 4. It's the easiest way to manage a room full of students if you have a little creativity. All classes have different and unique personalities. **As a result, you can alter the personality of a class by pinpointing disruptive students and relocating them to less distracting areas away from their friends and close to you.**

There seem to be three common behavioral problems that students exhibit:

- lack of self-control.
- inability to get along with peers.
- aversion to authority—particularly transference of problems with mom or dad to you, since you're the "parent" in the classroom.

Whatever the reason for the student's poor behavior, start by isolating him or her from the rest of the class—using corners of the room. The classroom, like society, has rules that can land people in "jail" for various offenses. This may sound harsh, but you're responsible for the welfare of the group, not the deviant—who has no right to prevent others from learning.

I remember a student who was getting a little out of control. I walked over to him and said, "Mr. J., sit over there, please!" "Why?" "You don't need to know the 'why' right now; just sit over there, please." After a few moments he got up and walked to the chair, mumbling his displeasure as he went. "Pardon me," I said, "I didn't quite hear that. ... Young man, you need to make a decision now: do as I ask, or leave! Your decision." The boy sat down. "Smart decision!" I said.

The next day I had a few quiet words with him and told him the "why." I explained I was leaning on him because I was disappointed with his lack of self-control. He understood and made an effort to improve. Don't feel obligated to respond immediately to a student's "why?".
Remember, you are the benevolent dictator!

To change behavior, you must make the student so uncomfortable that he or she wants to change. Usually within 2 months or so, the disruptive student will probably change his or her behavior, partly because of maturation, partly because of isolation from friends and partly because of the others' success with grades. This will further isolate the student emotionally and make him or her want to rejoin the group on your terms. In some cases, the best you will be able to do is simply control and not teach. Not pleasant, but again real! A parent once told me, "The only reason my son started to do his work in your class was because he realized that your head was harder than his!"

"The only reason my son started to do his work in your class was because he realized that your head was harder than his!"

Always watch for signs of a student's desire to rejoin the class. You might see his or her chair inch closer to friends, or the student might "accidentally" sit in the wrong seat after arriving to class. In either case, tell the student to return to the assigned spot with a few well-chosen words and then explain that the student has chosen his or her own consequences.

When looking back on my career over the years, some of my most enjoyable students started the year out in a corner. Remember, they are trying to see how far they can go! Stick to your standards for the class and you will be respected.

Classroom Arrangement

Another area to consider is how to arrange your room. There are many variations that the chairs in a room can take. But for your purposes as a beginner, have everyone face front and place your desk in the rear (best) or in the front. By placing your desk in the rear, they never know what you are doing, thinking or when you are watching. Also, by not allowing students to face each other in a classroom setting, you will get less spontaneous conversation and exert more control.

All students function better within clearly defined guidelines for behavior that create security. Despite what they say, all students want limitations.

It enables them to feel safe and secure. Also, with guidelines formally established, very few discipline problems should arise. The teacher must always look closely at what's going on, serving as instructor, advisor and referee. As the teacher, you provide a safe and secure learning environment for everyone, acting consistently over the long haul, while allowing students to make their own decisions.

TEACH SEZ:

An unstable student should be monitored closely. Jot down specific details of a student's poor behavior in your gradebook or separate notebook. **These anecdotal notes will be invaluable later when you find yourself sitting in a conference with a parent and guidance counselor or even principal** who asks, "Why did Johnny fail your class?" You may reply, "Well, he had eight classroom Fs, slept four times, missed eight assignments, zeros on four quizzes and a poor notebook." **Facts and figures usually aren't debated**. Keep in mind, some students may need specialized attention—from a resource teacher, tutor or special education assistant.

Detentions and referrals are easy ways to get the student out of class, but try to be judicious using these. Too many and the principal will question your ability to handle your own class. Principals respect teachers who don't send students out for every little thing. You are better off playing the detention game. If they don't show up, it's referral time.

Just remember the welfare of the class always comes first before any troublemaker's disruptions. Mr. Spock of *Star Trek* said it perfectly:

"Logic clearly dictates that the needs of the many outweigh the needs of the few."

Everyone cannot be saved from themselves. Concentrate your energies on those who want and deserve your help. The problem student will either change or, eventually, leave. Not nice to hear maybe, but true.

Remember, you're in charge. You have the authority to direct the class. When you roll out of bed every school morning, ask yourself, "What am I going to do for the students today? Not, what will they do to me today?" You must see yourself as the authority—anything less and you'll quickly become a doormat for kids to wipe their feet on. And they will. Keep your energy up. Without it, you'll succumb to the majority's wishes, which usually involves chaos and non-stop chatter. A 10-percent drop in your energy level will result in a 50-percent more difficult time controlling the class.

You should never have to repeat yourself more than three times. **The students are supposed to respond to you. Don't hand your authority over to them.** Try not to raise your voice repeatedly. It will only create student laughter and finger pointing. The fewer times you do, the greater the impact.

Nice kids hate extra work brought on by the bad behavior of their peers. The well-behaved students may become allies in your quest for class control and etiquette. Each class you teach will develop a unique personality with its own dynamics and active players trying to pull the strings. A strategy that works well in one class may fail miserably in another.

Sometimes peer pressure can work to your advantage while managing your classroom. Here's an example from my teaching experience:

It happened in a ninth grade class, actually a very immature class, when I had to confront two problems at the same time. I'd been having problems with a student who apparently had some personal issues to deal with. After two full quarters, he had barely a zero average. I isolated this boy by sitting him in the corner.

One day, while I was taking roll, I asked a student to get an admit slip from her first period teacher. She replied, "I ain't gonna!" The situation escalated because I wouldn't back down. I began walking the student out of the classroom when I heard mimicking remarks from the corner of the room. I knew who it was. At this point, the girl would not leave, so I called the vice principal to come down and escort her to the office.

The mimicking continued from the boy in the corner. The class began laughing. I whispered to the boy, while next to his desk, "Stop it." Because the class kept laughing, I said, "Since you've decided as a class to act as children and be influenced by a child, I will treat you that way. Open your books to page 419. Then write the questions and answer them (1 to 12) for 24 points due before the class ends! Furthermore, every time he (in the corner) says something, you as a class will have more work to do!"

One student yelled out, "That's not fair!" I replied, "You're absolutely correct, but you're encouraging his behavior. As a result, every time he makes his immature remarks, the class will work harder."

Wow. I was amazed at the number of people who started to yell, "Shut up" to the problem student. So much for classroom loyalty. As a result, the boy kept his comments to himself and actually did some work. I guess he didn't want to confront 29 angry students, some larger than he was!

Quoting my cousin who is an international motivational speaker for business: **People only change when they are made so uncomfortable that they want to change.**

SWARMING GNATS

Delays, Early-Outs:

Delayed school openings and early outs caused by bad weather are one of the perks of being a teacher. You sleep in and still get paid but, most importantly, the school is credited with an official "school day" that doesn't have to be made up.

Keep in mind it's a good idea to confront a student privately before or after class to avoid unnecessary humiliation of the student in front of his peers. Work within the limits of your personality. Sometimes humor works well, but never allow them to push you beyond your limitations.

Please be aware, the ice can get a little thin when issuing punishment assignments, so be prepared for flack. Have your justifications ready! Also remember, the event I have just described took place in the latter part of January, when the real division occurs between the maturing students and the ones who are left behind.

Never debate a student in front of a classroom.

Your decisions, as the benevolent dictator, are final and not to be challenged. Keep in mind, it is acceptable for a student to debate and argue with you about a topic or grade before or after class. Generally if a student has followed the correct procedure, I always try to find some extra points to help.

For example, "Mr. S., I have a problem with what you said." Or "Mr. S., I have a problem with the grade I received!" The potential argument becomes a discussion of fact and, in most cases, I try to find additional points for reinforcement if the students debate the topic correctly. Learn early who you can joke with and who you cannot. If a mistake was made, "OOPS, I'm sorry" will not harm your status in the students' eyes. Also, it is good for students to learn to say the same thing, instead of "It's not my fault."

Always put the students in a position to make both good and bad decisions. Even when reprimanding, give them a chance to choose. "I've asked you three times. Choose to sit where I told you or choose to leave." It's a set-up for a referral, and the student learns the valuable lesson of not confronting you.

At some point in your career, you will be openly confronted. Relax! These are great opportunities to establish yourself. Even though you will be upset or angry, you must maintain your external composure. Every word should be well chosen for effect. Remember, you will have to report what happened in writing. **Make sure you act professionally when interacting with even the rudest students, or your words and actions will come back to haunt you.**

TEACH SEZ:

Do not back down! You represent others in the class and you are a symbol of authority within the school. No one has the right to interfere with that. No matter how large a student is, he or she will still think like a child compared to you. Also, in any further administrative actions, **you will be viewed as the adult, someone capable of rational thinking.**

I remember a large male student once physically confronted me in class and suggested that we meet in the hallway. Even though part of me was beginning to move off the chair to head for the hallway to grant him his wish, I knew better as the adult in charge and followed the steps (listed on pages 47 & 48). Yes, I was annoyed and the flow of adrenaline was peaking, but I knew better than to act impulsively. The boy stormed out of my room and later was removed from my room and then expelled from the school for good. The point is this: keep impulsive reactions at bay and stay cool. Act professionally in volatile situations, and you will be rewarded. Remember, no matter how large students may be, they are still mentally children. Work with it!

Another story comes to mind when I was teaching night school. This class consisted of many students who were asked to leave the day school program for one reason or another. In fact, I usually enjoyed myself here because these students knew they were on the last rope. It was spring and the side door to the room was open. I began to hear a small ruckus between two girls. I told them to be quiet, and then a chair flew across the room and one of the students started screaming.

Pardon me, li'l Missy, but I'm the law in these here parts.

You must always think safety. So I ran and got myself in between the girls, while trying to fend off the larger one and telling the other one to go to the office. Of course, the one I sent to the office immediately thought I was blaming her rather than realizing I just wanted her out of the room. After a brief conversation, she left and now I could focus my attention on the other.

Meanwhile, the remainder of the class was laughing and looking quite amused by this outburst. However, they began to look a little concerned when the chairs began to fly again! I tried to calm the girl down and told her to step outside the room and relax for a few minutes. Just then another student shouted, "Are you finished now?" and the girl tore out the side door to the outside.

Realizing this was my chance, I shut and locked the outside door (safety first) and called the front office to notify them that "She is running loose!" Eventually they got her and later she received some counseling.

The following fall, I had her again in another class and, to say the least, I was apprehensive. She actually became a model student. So here is a prime example of providing safety to the class, giving them time to calm down, and allowing someone to mature and work through personal problems.

Another time, had I not maintained self-control, I might have ended my teaching career. The situation occurred in a boys' restroom. The room was off limits to students because of recent vandalism. When I walked in, I saw a boy cleaning up and looking in the mirror. I asked, "What are you doing in here?" He ignored me and attempted to walk past while brushing his shoulder against me. Adrenaline surged. I said, "What is your name, please?" as I blocked his path. Again he tried to get past me. Again, I blocked his path. He then began punching the air about 6 feet away from me, as if he were fighting me. Then he punched a commode stall. At this point, an administrator came in and took the boy up to the office. I immediately went to my room and wrote down a detailed account of what happened.

Twenty minutes later I was called to the office and confronted again by the same student in the principal's office. As I explained the situation, he, of course, denied it. I then elevated the stakes when I said I planned to file assault charges. Shortly thereafter, a state trooper entered and took the boy away in handcuffs. I was not threatened again for many years.

By the way, the student had to hire a lawyer. I had a representative of the State Attorney's office take the case because of my extensive notes on the incident. The case was eventually settled out of court with a 6-month PBJ statement. That was fine with me because of the lesson learned, not to mention the dollar cost of the boy's lawyer. However, the school board begged me to drop the charges because of the bad PR, and they were afraid they would lose. I knew better (I'm a realist). Once committed I had to complete the process if I wanted the message to the student body to stick: "Don't even think about assaulting a faculty member!"

Finally remember that it's always easier to loosen up classroom restrictions than to tighten them later. Many students see kindness as a trait to be exploited and will try to wear you and your rules down. This tactic is perfectly normal; just watch out. They can't help it; they're just being kids. Ninety-nine percent of them will grow out of it.

With lower academic tracts, I've found success for three reasons: One, I show them how to be successful (point sheet, how to take notes and the correct use of time and deadlines) and factor in the "maturation" rate. Two, I teach them to be reasonable. Because I also teach summer and night school, chances are they will see me again. And, finally, I eliminate all excuses for failure in advance so that the ultimate burden of responsibility falls on the student. The sooner they discover this, the more successful they become!

"Do as I ask and I can almost guarantee you an A or B. Mess with me and I'll not only fail you, but request your presence back with me again next year, so I can have at you again with more behavior modification!" Most of these kids might be slow, academically backward or even immature, but that does not mean they're stupid. This reasonable offer will be understood and they will respond to it by January of the school year unless the student has some psychological problem. Who wouldn't want to get an A or B with moderate work? As a result, there will be few behavioral problems.

Remember, the ultimate responsibility for everything in your room will be you. As a result, always think about safety and student-teacher interaction.

TEACH SEZ:

Steps for Normal Classroom Problems

1. Talk to the student politely.

2. Do not answer the question, "Why?"

3. Isolate the problem and present your options to the student.

4. If the student continues his misbehavior, write out a detention form (see Appendix, page 101).

    a. Say, "Show up for 10 minutes of detention *or* choose not to!"

    b. The student will either accept the punishment or throw away the detention form — which should result in a Referral.

5. If the disturbance continues, tell the student to "Get out!" Note the time and write up a referral.

6. Call parents ASAP to inform them of the problem. Remember Mr. Spock's words, "… the needs of the many outweigh the needs of the few."

7. Watch for changes in the behavior and maturity level of the student.

Steps to Consider in a Verbal Confrontation

1. Do not back down.

2. Calm the student.

3. Give the student available options.

4. Repeat the options again.

5. Tell the student to get out or do what you said.

6. Do not argue.

7. Begin writing detailed notes on the incident for the referral.

Steps to Consider for a Physical Confrontation

1. Turn sideways and keep an arm's distance away from the student.
2. Control the surroundings and the student.
3. Think about the safety of the other students.
4. Call for assistance.
5. Know the definitions of the terms *assault* and *assault and battery*.
6. Use whatever means necessary to restrain and protect the student, using minimum force.
7. Do whatever you need to do to protect yourself. Just remember you are still the responsible adult on the scene.

General Rules to Follow

1. Do not be a buddy to the students.
2. Hold students accountable for their decisions.
3. Never put yourself in a compromising situation with a student alone behind a closed door.
4. Keep detailed records and stay organized.
5. Use your time wisely.
6. Demand and command respect.
7. Always skew grades to the positive.
8. Isolate problem students.
9. Allow students to engage in the grading process.
10. You are the benevolent dictator. Act like it!
11. Prepare students for adulthood. You may want to use Mr. and Ms., Sir and Ma'am.
12. Avoid words such as "Shut up," "dumb," "stupid," etc.
13. Attack student's actions, not the student.
14. Always be consistent, fair, firm and relaxed.
15. Establish classroom policy and parameters on Day One. **Stick to them!**
16. Control comes first, then learning.
17. Compassion and kindness initially may be viewed as weakness.
18. Students want rules and limitations—for security.
19. Make students respond to you.
20. Never repeat yourself more than three times.

21. Teach the meaning of "reasonable."

22. Don't say it unless you intend to do it.

23. Make the right way easy and the wrong way difficult.

24. Understand differences between individual and group actions.

25. You begin and end class, not the bell.

26. Always follow-up situations that might occur during substitute visits.

27. Your classroom should mirror society with actions that have real consequences.

28. It isn't so much what you do or don't do. It's how you explain it.

29. Never lower yourself to the students' level. Make them rise to your level.

30. Pace yourself for the long haul!

31. Always return parent phone calls ASAP.

32. Avoid "Teacher Baiting" situations where one student plays off the actions of another.

33. Never turn your back on an unknown class.

34. Stay organized and stay ahead.

General Teacher Remarks

1. Thank you for sharing.

2. My name isn't "Man."

3. If you don't want to do it, don't. I'll just see you next year.

4. I've eliminated all excuses for your failure. Now the only way to fail is if you make the conscious decision to do so.

5. Option A or Option B, your choice! If it were me, I would choose Option A. Option B is not going to be to your advantage! Then follow through.

6. Be more concerned about what happens at your desk than what's happening over there!

Remember your ultimate obligation is to provide reasonable and adequate instruction, supervision, protection and supplies.

The Bottom Line:

1. Develop a *modus operandi* of your own based upon your personality and the experiences in your life.

2. Stay analytical and don't get emotionally involved when it comes to discipline.

3. Not all decisions have to be made at moment of infraction.

4. Help students cross the bridge to adulthood.

5. Despite problems, teaching is a rewarding profession.

6. Make sure the class knows your expectations.

7. The more battles you fight and win in September, the easier the remaining school year will be.

8. Know and learn the building's policies on student behavior.

9. Do not threaten—if you say it, do it!

10. Always be where you belong and be on time.

11. Maintain a positive attitude and facial expression.

12. Avoid leaving students unsupervised.

13. Keep a box of topic-related magazines and newspapers available for students who complete assignments.

14. Avoid the appearance of favoritism. (Likes and dislikes are normal; just don't act on them.)

15. Humor and firmness can go a long way.

16. Be a "sleeping lion."

7: Take Time to Reflect

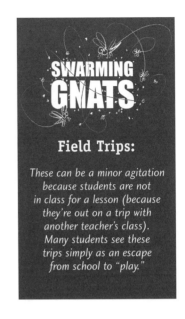

SWARMING GNATS

Field Trips:

These can be a minor agitation because students are not in class for a lesson (because they're out on a trip with another teacher's class). Many students see these trips simply as an escape from school to "play."

Try not to give assignments just to fill class time. This will happen on occasion when you're feeling wiped out or struggling with classroom management. Some classes can handle discussion better than others. Some students just need time to mature before respectful conversation can take place in an educational setting.

Remember, there's a time for work and a short time to relax before next class, as in 4 minutes.

During my first year of teaching, my last period class had 23 guys and three girls. It was rough. There were days where I had them read a chapter in class and answer questions in class on a worksheet I made up ahead of time. Many students ask, "Will this count?" Try not to be offended by this typical question. Remember, if no grade is entered in your gradebook, well, then it doesn't count to them—which leads to "off-task" time in class.

Some of my classes had 40 assignments in a quarter while others may have only had 10, depending on each class's maturity level. Try not to beat yourself up for not engaging the Socratic method daily. Do what it takes the first year to manage the class and teach at the same time. Go easy on yourself the first year if you fall back on pre-made worksheets. They are often rather boring, but they'll keep your head above water the first year! Just remember: no management, no learning.

As for meaningful standards, ask yourself, "What's the point of this?" when you prepare a lesson. If you're not convinced by what you tell yourself, go back to the drawing board. Believe me, students love asking, "What's the point of this?" They'll often add, "I don't need this. Who needs (you fill in the blank) to get a good job?" They're very utilitarian. **Try to have an answer in mind for why you do what you do. Try to be a reflective teacher**—that is, unless you want to be a hamster spinning a wheel into educational oblivion—wasting the students' time and yours.

FOOD FOR THOUGHT

Don't be afraid to try something new, something you're excited about—even if it's not in the defined curriculum. As long as you have a rationale, you'll be in fine shape. Without a nexus to the assigned curriculum, you may put yourself in a tight spot during an administrative observation.

Meaningful standards involve challenging the students, really making them think, as opposed to filling in worksheets like automatons. Provoke their minds. Sometimes that may mean saying something totally off the wall just for an opposing reaction. It's not hard to see who's engaged and who's not. Just look at their faces. Do they look bored? Glazed eyes?

Think again about what and how you're teaching.

The Bottom Line:

1. Ask yourself, "What's the point of teaching this material?"
2. Have a rationale for doing what you do.
3. Make them think. Don't let them just get by with bored expressions.
4. Be flexible, depending on each class's maturity and chemistry.

8: The Gradebook

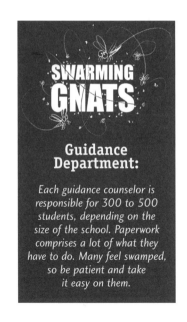

The most difficult thing for a new teacher—or any teacher, for that matter—to do is to develop a valid system of evaluation for the students. Even though many school districts have computerized grading, it's important to keep a written gradebook for backup and parent and administrative conferences, as well as for student usage.

I once had a principal who must have been petrified at the thought of bad grades in his building. At the end of every marking period, there was a long line of faculty members outside his office practicing explanations for their bad grade distribution. Conferences with this principal were usually an "informal" one-sided conversation that included the questions, "What's going on in your room?" "What are you NOT doing?" And the classic, "How can I help you correct YOUR problem?" The thought apparently never occurred to this administrator that the ultimate responsibility rests with the students. Dahh!!! The only way to diffuse this potential powder keg is to go on the offensive with a detailed gradebook as your weapon, thus proving that your grading decisions are based on student performance.

The key to success in working with all levels of students is to allow them to track their own scores (See Appendix, "Point Sheet," p. 100) and compare their records to the gradebook. I always allow students to work at their own pace and place their finished work into a Class Folder whenever they complete the assigned work. I do not collect the assignments; the responsibility rests entirely upon them. The Class Folder is corrected by me once or twice a week. Once students understand this system, most of them like it and behavioral problems decrease.

Students should be allowed to calculate their own grades from the gradebook, which creates an open atmosphere. The final grade is calculated by dividing the total possible points (denominator) by earned points (numerator).

It is also advisable to devise a method of extra credit, so students can make up points and recover from any bad judgment on your part. For example, you can have magazines in the room for students to read when they complete their regular assignments.

TEACH SEZ:

This idea will definitely help you maintain the high ground when conferring with students, administrators and parents. Nothing diffuses a tense situation quicker than being able to refer to a completely and accurately filled-in gradebook to support your assessment of a student's performance and the absence of any extra credit points. You won't be criticized for skewing grades to the positive. This will never change the facts: those who will, will; those who won't, won't.

I remember a student who actually was the slowest functioning student in all my years of teaching. What was interesting was that he wanted to do well but was just slow. When he had to function within normal timeframes, the situation was an absolute disaster with hardly any entries in my gradebook.

After a talk with his mother, we decided to disregard deadlines and let him work at his own pace. Sure enough, although the quality of his work was quite good, he still lacked the ability to finish all the assignments. But he honestly could get 70 percent with a little help from me (extra points for effort).

This example shows that **most kids can succeed in school, if they have decided to be successful.** Many kids, however, will choose to play the game of "excusism." This young boy proved to me that the student has to accept the ultimate responsibility to perform! As a result, look how he viewed his own achievement and boosted his self-confidence. Even more important, he learned about his limitations and how to overcome them.

As the adult and the professional, remember that it is always best to make the student responsible. This takes pressure off you. Students simply decide to do it or not to do it! "Mrs. Jones, what more can I do? I've made this as easy as I can and still teach the material!"

During the grading process, I have found that through the use of extended deadlines, many potential problems are avoided. By doing this, every student can get as much time as possible to complete the needed work. For example, I might say, "Next Tuesday all past work will be due! By this I mean any assignment that has not yet been turned in since the last deadline will be accepted. On Wednesday those same assignments will become zeros!" I've always found that a week before midterm and the end of the quarter is the best time to determine the percentage score. This gives me time to calculate averages and the student an opportunity to verify the numbers.

This system also teaches students about the meaning of deadlines. In your gradebook try drawing a red line down the page to indicate the deadline for the week due. It seems to work best to have a deadline every 3 weeks. It helps you manage your time. **Always notify the students 7 to 10 days in advance of your deadlines.**

Please take a moment and study the sample grade sheet on page 56. The gradebook may appear complex, but it contains all of the information you might need for a conference. The thing to note here is the use of the same color ink and the use of a pencil for attendance. In this way, each box can be used to keep a record of attendance and behavior as well as for academic scores.

Lastly please consider giving pop quizzes to students with the aid of student-generated notes. The advantage here is that quizzes do not have to be made up and are a reward for taking good notes. Also, consider allowing them to have an extra credit or make-up day.

Oh, I almost forgot, what will you do if students are sleeping during your class? Whenever they sleep, give them a zero for whatever assignment they were working on for that day and watch what happens!

As you can see, by the correct use of the gradebook, many problems—"the swarming gnats"—can be headed off in advance, not to mention preparing students for college and adult responsibilities! With a clear grading procedure in place, it's difficult to be second-guessed by students, parents and administrators.

An advantage of using a running total of points and a percentage grade is the addition of new students to your class. The best thing to do is to begin adding their point totals the day they arrive and create a separate percentage score using their individual possible total and not the class possible total. Again, this will put you in a positive light with the parents and create fewer long-term problems for yourself!

The Grading Balancing Act

There may be a few parents, however, who might not like this form of grading system because it puts too many demands and responsibilities upon the students at such an early age. Their usual negative remark will be as follows: "My son/daughter is too young to have to deal with this!"

That remark is the most common negative you will hear. Your rebuttal should go something like this: "Well, I understand. But, at what point will your child learn these needed skills? This year, next year ... perhaps in 10 years? I agree it's difficult for a child to learn how to manage his or her time. The sooner they do, the sooner their grades will improve. Learning how to learn is hard work! This is the best way to prepare your child for college and the workplace."

Rules for Grading

1. Be consistent and fair.

2. When in doubt skew grades to the positive.

3. Keep great records (grades, attendance, tardiness and behavior).

4. Allow students to have 5-10% of extra credit (to make up for quizzes and missed assignments).

5. Use total points denominator, earned points numerator.

6. Enforce deadlines for class work, notebook and reports.

7. First period only—record code number for absence (red ink).

8. Record grades in dark ink and attendance and miscellaneous in pencil.

9. Shutdown deadlines and grading at least one week before marking period ends to allow time for calculating quarter averages, plus verifying entries with students.

10. Allow students access to the gradebook with their point sheet.

11. Give students a chance to make up past work; use your best judgment here.

12. You may want to give a notebook grade depending on class level.

13. Don't be afraid to curve each class separately.

14. Try the following system:

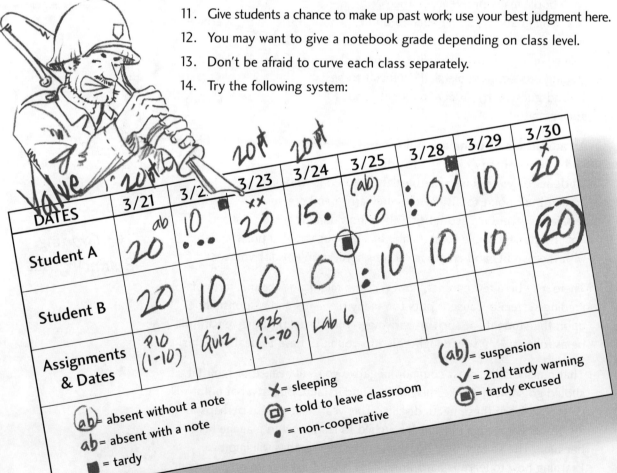

When collecting and evaluating long-term projects (i.e., term papers, reports), it is best to keep them secured until after the final grades are earned. This is in case a student wants to debate his/her paper and its effects on his/her final grade.

By following this grading policy, you will eliminate student excuses for failure. For example, a student might say, "I did that assignment." "Show me the work." "I did it. You must have lost it!"

If students are caught cheating, cancel their extra credit points enough to equal the point value on the cheated assignment plus a zero for the assignment. That will usually get their attention. There seem to be two general cheating methods—*direct*, i.e., student to student; and *indirect*, such as a student picking up notes or paper from the floor or slipping a note into a textbook before passing the book to another.

Cheating Techniques to Keep in Mind

1. Students will say their paper(s) got lost while in the Class Folder; do not throw out student assignments until after final grade.

2. Exchanging pens or pencils during a quiz, particularly if paper is graded in class by a peer.

3. They may attempt to imitate your handwriting on a paper.

4. Students may photocopy the text, saying they have taken their notes.

5. Students may make notebooks fatter with blank pieces of paper.

6. Answers may be written on hands or small pieces of paper, sometimes placed on their laps.

7. An attempt may be made to slip papers into the pile after the deadline. Don't be afraid to say, "I'm sorry, but it's too late; the deadline was…."

8. Students may attempt to alter or add scores to your gradebook.

9. Students will copy reports directly and totally from the internet.

10. Students will copy only the questions to assignments and not record the answers, hoping you don't see them.

11. Students will have answers in the bathroom during an exam.

The Bottom Line:

1. Be organized.
2. Be consistent and fair.
3. Err on the side of the positive; skew grades upward.
4. Keep an eye on everybody—even nice kids will cheat at times!
5. Encourage students to record/track their own grades.

9: Exams & Daily Evaluations

In our culture we speak of "holding schools responsible," but few have figured out that the students must be held accountable as well!

Some school districts are so paralyzed with fear over exam grades that seldom can a student fail unless he/she makes a conscious effort to do so. For example, prior to the end of the school year, I let my classes review for the final exam with a review sheet, my guidance and the use of about 7 days. I tell them, "if you cannot find something on the review sheet, please come up and ask me and I will be happy to give you the answer." Easy enough, right? Wrong!

Out of approximately 160 students, only three might come up to ask for help, while the others just talk and enjoy themselves during the class period. Furthermore, most of them report to class without a notebook, pen, text or paper. On the last day of the final exam review, I once stood before a class and told them, "I'm holding a copy of an old exam; what questions do you have?" I was not going to give them the questions, but I would help them focus on the topics to study. The hands went up and I began calling upon the students: "Can I go to the bathroom?" "What's for lunch?" "Is it going to rain this weekend?" "Can I borrow a pencil?" I just stood there in amazement. These questions were the culmination of the students' efforts for over a week and, sad to say, represented their interest.

Despite all efforts, exam day still arrived and the above students took the exam. Needless to say most of them scored in the 20 to 40 percent range, and I had to fail many of them for the school year. My attitude has always been to let them fail because they have made a conscious effort not to prepare!

But this school district, like many others, was so taken aback by the county's low test scores that they decided on the final day of school that teachers had to add a large "curve" to all the science exam results at the last minute,. Now, keep in mind, that many of us had already completed our final grade calculations and were waiting to be checked out by the boss.

This true story typifies the fear of letting the public know the truth: that a large percentage of their beloved sons and daughters do not care about academic success and do not study!!

SWARMING GNATS

Hall Passes:

Allow students access to the bathroom as long as they do not abuse the privilege. Remember, treat them like adults until they forfeit that individual right.

You might be asking yourself, why would a school district do that? The answer is really quite simple. It all boils down to funding and who wins in the local elections. It is far easier to deal with angry teachers than it is to deal with angry parents and an angry community.

Because many of these misguided administrators are followers of the "feel good" theory of education, the addition of the curves only validates the student's position of "why do it when I'll still pass one way or another?" Their actions only perpetuate this student attitude.

Personally I just can't understand why they are so frightened of telling the truth. It does not speak badly of them or the teachers; it simply means students have a different attitude concerning study and preparation than you had.

As a new teacher, there will be absolutely nothing you can do to change it, so don't even attempt it now. Even us old seasoned veterans are operating with one arm tied behind our backs on this issue. The funny thing is that this type of testing mentality will only get worse as more standardized tests are brought forth to justify the "feel good" concept of education.

Even us old seasoned veterans are operating with one arm tied behind our backs on this issue.

This doesn't mean that administrators are out to get you or that they are bad people. Their view of problems is quite different from those of us who work in the trenches. For example, let's say that you're in the trench armed with a rifle and a bayonet. You look over the edge of your trench and see the enemy breaking through the wire barrier and heading toward you. After a flash moment of panic, you yell for help at the top of your voice.

The administrators recognize your situation and acknowledge your call from a hill to the rear where they are surveying the entire battlefield and deciding how best to win the campaign!

The fact is that the farther up you go in the chain of command, the less real accurate information is available from the trenches. A teacher generally makes decisions based on immediate need; an administrator makes decisions based on trends, budgets and projections and often has a big picture perspective.

By the way, going back to the original story: my immediate boss was also peeved. Because of the added curve on the final exams, a few seniors who had already failed and missed graduation, now theoretically passed the failed courses. What do you say to those kids' families? Perhaps give them the beginning date for summer school?

The bottom line here is that **success must come from within and it cannot be regulated by counties, states or the powerful federal government.** If kids do not want to learn, no power on earth can make them do it!

So here is your challenge: You do not want merely to survive but to rekindle that flame of interest within students, without lowering yourself or your standards. And whatever you do, don't beg them to perform and—and—and—and "keep good records!"

The Bottom Line:

1. Allow students to decide between failure and success.
2. Keep track of numbered tests when giving state or county exams.
3. Provide a review sheet.
4. Designate class time for student preparation for the final exam.

10: Parents

Sometimes one of the most frustrating aspects of the teaching profession is working with parents. Parents can be individuals desperately searching for help or individuals who simply want a current update of their child's performance. In both cases, be polite and welcome their input and desire to help, even though they can be pushy at times.

Speaking of pushy, I remember a mother who was always polite and interested in her son's progress but eventually moved into the realm of being a total pest! I used to dread the announcement over the PA: "Mr. S., please report to the office for a phone call." Ninety-eight out of 100 times, it was this parent! Yes, she had a perfect right to contact me for an update, but she began to interfere with the other families represented in the classroom. This person became so bold that she actually tried to get grades changed by making up a lot of really great excuses for her son's total lack of academic concern and effort. It got so bad that she even began to annoy the vice principal in charge of her son and the boss himself.

"Mr. S., please report to the office for a phone call. It's your favorite parent, Mrs. You-Know-Who..."

Even here, the administration used tact and allowed her to blow off steam. To this day, I still find her to be a nice person, just overly pushy. This would be especially true in parent-teacher conferences where I had to be careful to maintain control by keeping accurate records of her son's behavior and levels of work.

The parent-teacher conference will be no problem if you handle it properly. When introducing yourself, use your full name, "Hi, I'm Phil Jones, your son's English teacher," and shake the parent's hand. This immediately sets the tone and creates an atmosphere of respect and cooperation. Remember, up to this point, the parent has only heard the child's side of the story. Give the parent some time to vent if the child's story has been a negative one.

The reason for blowing off steam may be the parent's frustration about the lack of his or her ability to help the child. Don't take it personally. Most parents understand that the child, not the teacher, holds the key to success.

This reminds me of another story. I went into a conference with a father concerned about his daughter's poor grade. He was convinced that I

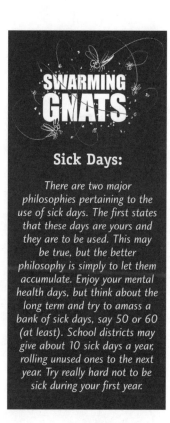

didn't like the child and had tried to sabotage her success. After allowing him time to express his thoughts, I began to counter by explaining my grading policy and enumerating the number of times this student was off task. I then invited the father to view my gradebook after giving an explanation of my grading policy.

With that, the chilled atmosphere of the conference began to change immediately, and his frustration shifted from me to his daughter. Putting the onus on the student, I asked the girl, "Isn't that right? Don't you sometimes talk with (whomever)? Don't I call you Miss or Ma'am in class?"

At this point the father was momentarily lost. With the facts established, I said to him, "Mr. Smith, you seem like a concerned parent. What can I do to help? What if I allowed her to go back and make up her past work? Would that help? What can we do to help her be successful?" By the end of the year, this parent was one of my strongest supporters. The following year I had his daughter again for another course. She not only got an A but enjoyed being in the class.

This is a clear example of how keeping accurate records on every student curtails parent-teacher tension in a conference. **Few parents choose to debate or argue with facts, figures and dates.**

Lastly remember that a large percentage of students live in a one-parent household. As a result, some parents come to these conferences with more than one suitcase of emotional baggage.

Parent Telephone Conferences

Always remain in control and professional while speaking to a parent. And present the facts. Telephone calls usually aren't stressful if you have a game plan in mind before dialing. Key words or notes jotted down for reference may be helpful, particularly if you're feeling nervous.

Always give the parent time to express frustration but don't tolerate verbal abuse. At no point does a parent have a right to be abusive to you. If the conversation gets out of control on the telephone or in a conference room, just say: "Excuse me. I'm sorry. I don't have to listen to this. I'd be happy to talk about this when you're more rational." Report incidents like this to your immediate supervisor, before they get a telephone call from an irate parent. Your principal will usually be supportive.

The script for a typical phone conversation might go like this:

Teacher: Mrs. C.: Hi, this is Phil Jones from CHS. I'm your son's science teacher and I'm returning your call.

Mrs. C.: Oh, I'm so glad you called. I've just been wondering what's been going on in your class. I've looked at the midterm notice and he had an F on it. Michael has been telling me that you didn't count a number of his assignments. Is that so?

Teacher: Mrs. C., I'm glad to finally be able talk with you about Michael. Did he tell you that the deadline for all of that work was September 20th, but he gave it to me on the 27th? Also, did he tell you that he received 12 classroom Fs in the last 4 weeks for not using the class time?

Mrs. C.: What do you mean? My son usually does what he's supposed to do.

Teacher: I realize that, but here at school with friends around, many students get distracted. But that's neither here nor there. What can we do to help Michael succeed?

Mrs. C.: I can't watch him all the time, and I can only go by what he says. Who has he been hanging around with? What can I do?

Teacher: I've noticed a change in his personality. Take a look at his point sheet.

Mrs. C.: His what?

Teacher: His point sheet, the record of all his assignments and grades in class. Remember, I'm trying to prepare him for college, not just spoon-feed him.

Mrs. C.: I think he's too young to be given this much freedom with his classwork.

Teacher: Would you prefer him to learn it now or wait until he's in the 12th grade, or perhaps never learn it? I agree it is difficult for him, but the sooner he learns to take on the responsibility, the better prepared he will be. Trust me! How about making an appointment with his guidance counselor? Then we all can meet to take a look at Michael's grades and come up with a plan of action to help your son.

Mrs. C.: Well, thank you. That sounds like a good idea. How do I contact his counselor?

"Can we try it again, please, and this time with a little more feeling …"

During the phone conversation, notice how a few words or statements have a calming effect and create an ally and not an adversary. Most telephone calls are similar to this.

Always take notes during phone calls for your records.

Back-to-School Night

Here at last is your chance to view the parents and for them to see you. All they know is what their children tell them, and hopefully a positive reputation precedes you!

Try to include the following topics, which will surely cover the 8-10 minutes you have to speak to the parents:

1. Grading policy.
2. Point Sheet. (Parents' homework is to check it and follow the point accumulation.)
3. Explain action-reaction theorem of student-teacher interaction.
4. Philosophy to help students grow into successful adults.
   A. To prepare them for college and the workplace:
      1. Notetaking   3. Listening skills (pop quizzes)
      2. Point Sheet   4. Deadlines
   B. Prepare for life after high school:
      1. Use of Sir and Ma'am / Mr. & Miss, etc.
      2. Politeness
   C. To show them how to be successful:
      1. Grading
   D. To create a safe classroom for making mistakes and learning from them.
   E. To learn the subject matter and its application.

Why is learning the subject matter last on the list? Simply because a student who can do A B, C and D can learn any subject matter.

Rules for Parent Interaction

1. Return phone calls within 24 hours, same day if possible!
2. Allow them time to express their frustration.
3. Be prepared with good academic and behavior records.

4. Give them a strategy (point sheet), so they can be involved in the grading process.

5. Do not take verbal abuse.

6. Always invite them to view your gradebook.

7. Create a partnership, not an adversarial relationship.

8. Explain your grading and classroom philosophy.

9. Admit mistakes.

10. Be flexible with each situation.

Parents Want...

1. Honesty and fair dealing.

2. Help to relieve guilt and frustration.

3. Contacts by telephone.

4. Reassurance.

5. A doable plan for their child's success in class.

Things to Say and Words to Use with Parents

1. Now what would you like me to do to help?

2. We...

3. What can you tell me to help me make a decision?

4. Yes, your information does make a difference!

5. Please feel free to contact me.

6. I'm sure that together we can work through the problem!

7. Is there anything else I should know?

8. I'm sorry you feel that way; however...

9. I can't make it any easier than it already is.

The Bottom Line:

1. Learn "**Rules for Parent Interaction**" above.

2. Learn "**Things to Say and Words to Use with Parents**" above.

11: Administration & Supervision

One of the most important factors in your success as a teacher will be your relationship with your immediate boss, the principal. There are usually two levels of administration: the building supervisor, the reality-based individual, and the headquarters-type administrator—the theorist. The primary difference is how problems are viewed. One level deals with the everyday operations within the building, while the other must contend with funding, politics and educational theories.

With this in mind, let's take a look at the people who will impact your career. Very early on, you must be able to "size up" the administration under which you will work. The main question that must be asked or at least researched is, "Do you/they believe in 'feel good' education or in "reality-based" education? Reality-based beliefs have roots in traditional values where people earn what they deserve. On the other hand, "feel good" education has no major root system except for the belief that everyone has a valid excuse and must feel good about themselves. Believe me, you do not want to be in a situation or in a building that does not support you. If your principal begins talking about "everyone is equal" (students and faculty), watch out!

What is a "feel good" administrator? This may be a person who blames you for not motivating the student rather than the student for not studying. Or perhaps the administrator views you as the aggressor and the child as the victim in a dispute, rather than looking at the student's misbehavior.

I clearly remember a situation that will help clarify this issue. There was once an up and coming vice principal who was a great follower of the school's sports program and knew many of the athletes. Just my luck, I had a physically imposing basketball player who enjoyed acting like a fool during my class time. One day I accepted his challenge and made him sit in the corner by himself. He didn't like his new seat, of course, and let everyone known about it. Myself, I always rather enjoy knowing this type of student is miserable because that means the rest of the class can concentrate on learning without feeling threatened by interruptions.

After this event, I was walking past the vice principal's office and he called me in. After a few moments of chit-chat, he asked me why the

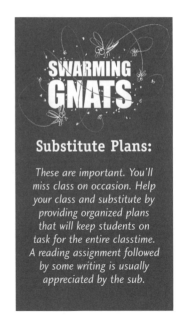

SWARMING GNATS

Substitute Plans:

These are important. You'll miss class on occasion. Help your class and substitute by providing organized plans that will keep students on task for the entire classtime. A reading assignment followed by some writing is usually appreciated by the sub.

basketball player was sitting by himself in the corner. I explained what was going on—accurately and without emotion.

What do you think this administrator said to me? Was it, "Gee, Phil, you did a great job protecting the class from this disruptive student"? Wrong!! Would you believe that his greatest concern was on the potential damaging effect to the child's ego: "You'll destroy him!" I won't tell you my response! But here was "feel goodism" at its best, where the needs of the individual far outweigh the needs of the group. By the way, the student in question continued to stay in the corner for the duration of the school year, in spite of pressure from the administrator.

Within the entire field of education, no one is under more stress and pressure than the high school principal. The principal must represent the local Board of Education and the implementation of the contract, as well as interact with parents, the community, students and the faculty, including support staff. Also, the principal is ultimately responsible for school finances and building maintenance. Everything that happens on campus rests on the principal's shoulders.

As a result, administrators are always interested in people who can bring the school good publicity and positive PR. In short, **appearance and perception are important!** Furthermore, principals want employees who are fast thinkers, creative, independent and, above all, able to manage their classrooms.

 **TEACH SEZ:** **Understand that a relationship exists between the front office and your classroom, a symbiotic one, where the success of both depends upon each other.**

The following rules will ensure your success:

1. Always remain loyal to the position of the principal. People come and go. Everyone has likes and dislikes, but the position of principal should always have your respect.

2. Let the boss know that he/she can always count on you for extra help.

3. Your personal word is your bond. Don't violate it!

4. Do whatever you can to lighten the load.

5. Admit mistakes.

6. Principals want to know whom they can rely on—be one of them.

7. Protect your boss from being blindsided. If an event occurs let the boss know ASAP, so he/she has time to think out the best response.

I remember once, during a conflict with a student, I misread the situation. The student wanted to go to the nurse, and I denied the request because he had a long history of exaggerating. He said he was sick and that his mother would pick him up. As it turned out, I was wrong and reluctantly let the kid go to the office. During my break I was going to let the boss know of my mishandling the situation and my desire to call the parent to apologize. No sooner did I open my mouth, when he asked, "Was her name Mrs. D?" That's how fast things can happen. By the way, I called, explained the situation and she eventually became an ally!

The principal projects his control over the building in one of two ways: like a lion or like a fox. The lion philosophy of administration works primarily with daily problems much like the lion itself. They both believe in strength, head-on tactics, intimidation and confrontational skills in order to achieve their goals. Like teachers, principals must work within their own personalities in order to be genuine and real. In some cases, these people are easier to work with than the more clever, multi-faceted fox, because you know precisely where you stand in your relationship with them. Confrontational behavior doesn't necessarily mean that the teacher or administrator is without compassion or feelings.

Unfortunately lions may actually become brutish Neanderthals, often grunting as a form of communication, instead of projecting a joyful "Good morning." But luckily these cases are quite rare. I don't believe that they are naturally mean people, but the stress of the job and philosophy of task orientation can eventually wear down one's good nature. Morale and productivity can only decline sharply under their leadership. Very little can be accomplished here, except your personal survival.

The smart modern administrator (fox) works with you in a give-and-take relationship governed by respect. Morale soars, as well as productivity and spirit. Reporting to work each day becomes a reasonably pleasant experience. Remember the goal of any administrator is to strengthen the school by strengthening you. Only the methodology will vary.

The science of administration is defined as "getting people to do what you want them to do because they want to do it." As a result, all strategies are fair.

Observations (See Appendix, page 103)

During your teaching year, you will be observed at least once a quarter, but more likely two or three times. What's an observation? What are administrators looking for? What is their purpose? Most smart administrators already know more about you by walking past your room every day than by having a formal observation.

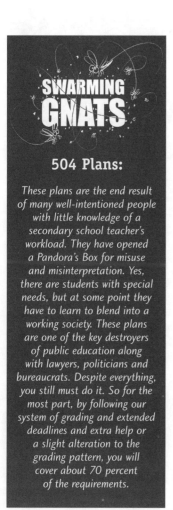

In order to answer these questions, let's begin with the first question. What's an observation? All teachers are officially and unofficially observed throughout the school year. The longer you stay with a certain school, the less you will be observed because of your reputation, success and the administrator's limited time. As a matter of bookkeeping, however, the principal and Board of Education must be able to justify your continued employment by formal observations and follow-up evaluation.

Each building administrator has a slightly different idea of what is vital to your success and, in turn, the school's success. Therefore, get to know the senior faculty members in your new building or listen to conversations in the teacher's lounge.

All administrators want to see some kind of control and teacher-student interaction within the classroom. Below is a list of five main items that the new teacher should concentrate on during the first year:

1. Try to include all students in the lesson.
2. Make the lesson's concept clear and appropriate to the specific level of the class.
3. Be sure to have an official opening and closing to each lesson.
4. Be organized and have a method for your management of the classroom.
5. Always demonstrate active student-teacher interaction.

Be sure to examine the sample observation form included in the Appendix on page 103.

In order to cover the above items during your observation, try to master these techniques:

1. Move around the room and look over the shoulders of students while they work.
2. Allow students to have easy access to you and your gradebook.
3. Promote a relaxed but controlled classroom atmosphere.
4. Allow students to work in pairs.
5. Share smiles and a few words with students during the class activity beyond the lesson.
6. Keep objectives on the board.
7. Always have some warm-up activity to keep the class occupied while you perform normal administrative chores such as attendance checking.

Referrals (See Appendix, page 102)

The last area that we need to talk about in this chapter is the dreaded referral. How you write them and how many you send will have a direct effect on your success or failure in your new profession. It should always be considered the last resort. From the view of the vice principal, it represents an additional workload and gives them a basis to form a negative opinion about you. Administrators do not like to see a lot of frivolous referrals. But keep in mind: if a student deserves a referral, don't hesitate to send him out. **The first secret to writing a successful referral is to always put the administrator in a win-win situation. They'll love you for it!** By this I mean to set up the referral like a one-way street leading to a destination by building the case.

EXAMPLE A:

1. I asked the student to stop talking and said "sit down" three times.
2. Student began to question my authority to give directions and said, "_____."
3. I asked the student a fourth time to sit down and stop talking as the student continued to argue aggressively.
4. I then told him to sit down and begin work or get out.
5. Student walked out at _____ p.m.

Now put yourself in the administrator's position as you read this situation. What else can you do except discipline the student for insubordination?

EXAMPLE B:

1. Detention notice given on 11/5 for 11/6.
2. Student said, "I'm not going."
3. No show for detention on 11/6—no prior arrangement made.

EXAMPLE C:

1. The student has been a continuous source of disruption from across the room (talking, laughing, etc.).
2. The student continuously attempts to gain attention and prevent other students from completing their assignments.
3. This student has not responded to prior administrative actions (moved seat two times and two detentions).
4. Sent out at ___ p.m. after student refused to follow my directions.

Again, notice how the words in the above examples "build the case"! This is important if some parent can't believe her/his angel would ever be in such a mess. Some parents end up being defensive, simply because they feel the referral is a negative thing.

What really happens when a referral is written? When the vice principal receives the item, it usually goes into a stack with other referrals and he/she has a limited amount of time for each person in order to expedite the referral back to you (24-72 hours). When they read a referral that builds a case, their job becomes easier.

The student typically comes into the vice-principal's office and is confronted by the VP in charge of that graduating class. Once there, the VP reads over the referral and passes judgment after calling the child's parents and discussing the situation. The interaction and resolution is entered into a student logbook for future reference.

The second great secret to writing referrals is in the use of key eye-catching words that send red flags to the reader. The correct choice of words is perhaps the greatest tool a teacher can use when issuing a referral.

Here is a list of effective word choices, which will usually get an active response from an administrator. Of course, when sending a referral, always have ample documentation to back it up in your gradebook. Finally keep a record of all detention and referral forms.

Here are some words that will strengthen your referral writing. Be sure that your interpretation of these words is similar to your administrator's!

1.	Distracting	7.	Insubordinate
2.	Inciting	8.	Disrespect
3.	Refusal	9.	Continuous
4.	Prolonged	10.	Endanger
5.	Interfering	11.	Aggressive
6.	Confronting	12.	Threaten
	13. Walked Out		

Thinking About a Promotion?

Now that you're a teacher, you may want to consider a promotion. What does a promotion mean as a teacher? To begin with, you become a vice principal. Vice principals are the workhorses of the building. You will find them on the job before you arrive and when you leave at the end of the day. They carry out the wishes of the principal and answer to him/her for mistakes.

Earlier I spoke of the fox, lion and the brutish form of management. Imagine being under that Neanderthal we spoke of earlier with no place to hide! In contrast, the better the school and working environment, the more praise the principal will get for his/her future résumé. Even though the vice principal post is an entry-level position, many people can make a career out of it. Most high school administrators work an average of 60 hours per week, including nights. Consider yourself lucky if you have a real good one.

Let's ask the big question: "How can I become an administrator?" Generally you need about 5 to 7 years of successful teaching to begin to consider it, and you must have a master's degree with a certification in administration and supervision (A&S). If a district really wants you, it will make deals or conditions for your new employment. An A&S certificate is like getting your teaching certificate, but it has two levels. You must generally sit through an administrative clinic, where administrators evaluate your performance in role playing situations.

Many schools like to promote from their coaches and athletic directors. Why? I haven't a clue except for the possibility that these people are used to interacting with the public. Another way to be sought after is to develop a track record as a volunteer, club sponsor and extra helper whenever possible.

Even before the interview begins, the evaluators are already searching for unique qualities that the job opening at the school requires. For example, the job may call for a female because the other administrators are male. Or they might need a good public relations person to complement the task-oriented front office or vice versa to create a balanced administrative staff. Sometimes jobs may be filled even before the interview process even gets started. Normally it takes at least three interviews to achieve your goal. When you are asked questions during the actual interview, the evaluators will often award a point value from 1-10 for each response.

If you enjoy having responsibility and enjoy working hard with a sense of satisfaction, this could be the job for you. Remember that you must possess some writing ability. Also, you must have good PR and political skills. When those annoyed parents knock at your door, saying their child is a perfect angel and would never etc., etc., etc.—you will begin to earn your pay.

The best job going could be that of a vice principal in a middle school or elementary school simply because the hours are often less, and there are few nighttime activities compared to a high school.

Oh, one last thing, the principal's salary is based upon the size of the faculty and responsibility factor. If you achieve this lofty goal, be sure to factor in gym time so you rule like a fox and not like a stressed-out Neanderthal!

Characteristics of a Good Administrator

1. Cheerful.
2. Organized.
3. Supportive.
4. Balanced—humanistic (50%) vs. (50%) task-oriented.
5. Enjoys interactions with people.
6. Feels a total commitment to an organization.
7. Thrives on hard work.
8. Able to handle discipline and objectives.
9. Friendly.
10. Outgoing personality; introverts need not apply.
11. Able to handle pressure and stress.
12. Multi-talented.
13. Patient.
14. Must understand the total picture and be able to communicate well.
15. Tactful.

The Bottom Line:

1. Build a positive and professional relationship with your principal.
2. Learn your principal's managerial style .
3. Prepare interactive/engaging lessons that score high on observation days.
4. Write specific referrals using choice "key" words.
5. Brace yourself for heavy responsibility if you are thinking promotion to administration.

12: Having a Life

Your first year of teaching will be incredibly time consuming. As an academic English teacher, I averaged 80-hour work weeks my first 2 years on the job. Years 3 and 4, I knocked down to 70-hour weeks. Years 5 and 6 turned into 55-hour weeks, thanks to assigning very few essays. Many of the classes were honors classes; a few, general.

The workload will get easier over the years. And remember, different courses demand different amounts of preparation and grading.

Don't be surprised to find yourself grading papers on weekends and evenings. And then there's lesson planning. If you have three or four preparations, you will find yourself performing a juggling act— keeping track of what each class is doing. One day may consist of four different discussions about four different novels. Keeping all that information readily available is not easy.

Some teachers try to grade papers during class, particularly if a group of students is engaged in an in-class activity. How does a teacher keep an eye on the class during an activity and pay attention to grading at the same time? It doesn't work, unless what you're grading is mindless student work. And if you deem it as mindless, you may want to ask yourself why you assigned it in the first place!

I find that grading papers during a film activity, however, is a great way to utilize my time and give the students a break from the normal class routine. It also lightens my homework load.

The All-Consuming Time Monster

To teach well takes time.

To grade well takes time.

To lesson plan well takes time.

So where do you find time to have a personal life? How do you keep the resentment at bay when some of your colleagues and friends shout "TGIF" on Friday as you load papers to grade into a Barnes and Noble bag?

First, you must ask yourself, "Why did I choose to teach?" If you really want to impact lives, you will devote a lot of the school year to your students. Many of my students still keep in touch with me. Letters, e-mails, phone calls have continued years after they left the class. **Students see who invests in them and who just punches the time clock.**

FOOD FOR THOUGHT

SWARMING GNATS

Bus Passes:

Keep a stack in your desk for students who stay after school for extra help or in a group you sponsor. Some bus drivers will turn kids away if they don't have a pass.

Keep in mind that you have the summer off and 2 weeks off for Christmas break. How many jobs give you 12 weeks off a year? And in the summer you can travel or pursue other hobbies. Do not underestimate the value of the huge chunks of free time.

Teaching is all-consuming during the school year. If any teacher tells you something different, question whether or not they're really making a difference. I put photos of Glacier National Park in Montana on my podium as a little reminder of my summer plans. Getting through a difficult class will be more than worth it when you're driving the "Going to the Sun" Road in Montana in July.

Of course, there are many rewards in teaching during the school year. Reminding yourself of even the small victories will help keep you going. Treasure positive student feedback; hold onto cards of gratitude— reminders that your work is not in vain—that you're more than "just a taskmaster" for students who say they hate school.

If you don't like children or adolescents, don't go into teaching. That may sound like a no-brainer, but you will find people in the profession who clearly don't want to be there and don't seem to care much about kids. Don't make yourself a prisoner to your own bad decisionmaking to become a teacher if you really don't want to do it!

So, how do you have a life and teach at the same time? First, realize that spending time helping students, both academically and as a role model of character, is having a life. Teaching is a noble profession; never mind the cynics who mock that idea. Try not to resent spending a lot of time helping others. That, in large part, is what teaching is all about.

I try to set aside at least one day a week, usually Sunday, as a non-work day because the mind needs a break from school ... for emotional well-being and to avoid burnout. I might have to work 6 or 7 hours on a Saturday, but knowing Sunday will be free really helps my morale.

Now for those of you thinking, "What? Having Sunday free helps your morale?" Just wait. The paperwork will flow in. When you have an average of 170 students a day (which I have had since starting teaching), think of the paperwork. You really can't until you get in it and find yourself trying to avoid the ever-growing tidal wave of "things to get done."

Make friends with at least one or two other teachers. They'll understand what you're saying as you express your exhaustion and frustration. People in the outside world don't get it. They can't imagine what it takes to teach well. I certainly never imagined what it would take.

Value the time you spend with and for the students. Oh, and before you start your first year of teaching, promise yourself to come back for a second. The first year is like no other in terms of the workload! Just think how many professions give the same responsibilities to the first-year employee and the 30-year employee? Teaching does. There is no increase in responsibility. It's all there from day one! Brace yourself accordingly!

The Bottom Line:

1. Remember teaching is a noble profession.
2. The school year is often all-consuming. Think "summer" if it helps.
3. Make a few teacher friends. You're going to need them.
4. Being overwhelmed is OK during the first year.
5. Save positive feedback from students.
6. Seek help from a mentor teacher in your building.
7. Keep your life compartmentalized.
8. Maintain a master desktop calendar.
9. Stay ahead of schedule.
10. Every morning make a "must do list" for that day.
11. Utilize school time to the max.

13: Feeling Pretty Stressed

Stress goes with the territory. No matter how hard you may try to avoid it, the day will come that you feel the hair starting to stand up on the back of your neck. But you want to be an effective teacher and keep your job, so...

Stay cool in the classroom!

When the anger boils and you say in your mind, "I don't have to put up with this job! How many college-degreed people put up with this kind of crap?" ... find a place to vent. Try to squeeze in a physical outlet such as walking, jogging, swimming, something! Externalize the frustration with physical activity to purge your system of the student attitude residue that lingers long after class ends.

Finding friends who understand is essential. You will need to vent to them, "Drain the boil" as one of my colleagues would say. If you don't have a place to voice your frustrations with a class, the anger will just continue to build inside you—leaking out during class in passive-aggressive and sarcastic comments. Pink Floyd's refrain, "We don't need no education," may reverberate in your classroom, but that doesn't mean you have to add your "dark sarcasm" to the mix. It only makes things worse.

Some days you may just want to wing it in the classroom with minimal preparation. Proceed at your own risk. Poor preparation will only set yourself up for an even more chaotic classroom, and your feelings of helplessness and powerlessness may escalate. So, whatever you do, don't walk into a classroom without a solid lesson plan or without alternative backups.

I keep a file cabinet full of good videos—some educational, some just plain fun—to use if I'm feeling frazzled.

Sometimes the class just needs a breather from the struggle for control with the teacher.

Use full-period videos judiciously. When you're on the edge of quitting the job or you start saying, "I hate them" in your mind, that's a good time to grab a video and decompress. You may want to invest in a cheap VCR for your classroom. You can't always rely on your school's media center to have one available.

When the stress builds —and it will — vent to understanding friends (usually another teacher), exercise and keep your video collection well stocked.

The Bottom Line:

1. Make teacher friends for support.
2. Keep a good video collection with lesson plans on hand for mental hygiene days.
3. Don't wing it (without a lesson plan); it will only make your life more difficult.
4. Exercise your feelings out.
5. Establish a routine that will reduce stress.
6. This, too, shall pass.

SWARMING GNATS

Custodial & Cafeteria Staffs:

Be friendly with these workers. They directly affect your life in ways you may not even realize. Christmas gifts to these employees (and the principal) are a good idea. Stay genuine and remember the golden rule!

Sometimes the class just needs a breather from the struggle for control with the teacher.

14: Summer & Night School Gigs

The best gigs in any school system are Summer School and Night School programs. Most teachers would say that I'm nuts for even thinking this, and their opinions might be correct. But I have found that these students are easy to work with once you have established control.

Many of these students have discipline or attendance problems during the normal school year. As a result, they know that this is their last chance. Also, in many cases, discipline problems cease once the learning atmosphere has been changed and established.

Both programs present an excellent chance to make good extra money with little effort and supervision. Once an administrator knows you are capable and competent, you are, for the most part, left alone. However, I always keep them informed of any upcoming problem that I might foresee. Remember, complaints from students or parents will ultimately be directed to you, with the administrator acting as referee.

So, how do you take on summer school or night school? To begin with, you must be strong in your beliefs of tough love, strong in your organizational skills and strong in classroom management. You might be asked to teach multiple subjects in the same room during the same block of time to different levels of students.

This might sound impossible, but it can work to your advantage. The best strategy is to list the daily assignments on the board for each student area and have the students participate in an "independent study" program. Here everyone is working at his or her individual pace, aware of the midterm and final deadlines for classwork, reports and notebooks. Don't forget to use a total point accumulation as a grading system.

Each hour of assignments should represent one lesson. Because most summer school and night school courses are 3 hours per day, you can see that each day would represent 3 days of classes. Always have extra

If you handle these summer and night school situations, you will be rewarded with extra dollars and extra praise.

assignments as backup in case there are discipline problems or the students complete their tasks. Remember it's difficult, at best, for adults to remain seated for 3 hours, let alone a group of adolescents.

I always have the students work about an hour and a half before a break. Then I show them a film or have them in some kind of group activity. It's OK to allow the class to decide when they should take a break. As a rule, the more basic and general a student is, the more the need arises to have short breaks, perhaps 5 minutes per hour.

I feel that any student who sits through summer school or night school, has not created problems and has made some effort deserves to pass with at least a 60 percent. As a result, be sure that the student has a solid grade prior to the final exam. A good rule to follow is for the classwork to represent 80 percent and the exam to represent 20 percent. The final exam, therefore, takes on a secondary role. For example, if a student had a 100 percent on all work from the class and did not take the final exam (0 percent), he or she would receive an 80 percent as a final grade.

When working summer school, follow the rules already mentioned in this book and you'll be just fine. Also, remember to keep a hard copy of your grades, even though some school districts use a computerized grading system. I always enter "totals" into the system and keep the daily details in my gradebook for reference.

If you handle these summer and night school situations, you will be rewarded with extra dollars and extra praise. Administrators smile kindly on those teachers who can handle "alternative" classroom environments.

The Bottom Line:

1. Don't tolerate any misconduct.

2. You are a benevolent dictator.

3. Use a point system and independent study for grading.

4. Keep excellent records.

5. If needed, find and act on disruptive students to reinforce your discipline from the first day.

6. It's okay to feel empathy towards the students.

15: Financial Matters

The Double-Edged Sword

Some teachers always complain about their paychecks. I guess they do have an argument when compared to government and private business. Often they fail to understand that this compensation represents only 10 months of actual employment. During this 10-month period, there are 10 to 14 days off for Christmas, 3 to 7 days off for spring break, a couple more days off at Thanksgiving, not to mention inservice days and personal leave.

Most certainly, everyone wants more money, myself included, and this will be happening in the years to come—simply because future salaries must be higher to attract and retain good teachers from a young work force anxious for the finer things in life. During the next decade, a teacher's certificate could end up bringing in top dollars, compared to some government and business salaries.

Keep in mind that after teaching 5 to 7 years, you may feel trapped in the school system. That's because a mortgage, a baby and a new car could lock you into that paycheck you're bringing home. It is often difficult to quit the profession once you're in for several years. Think about that early on in your career.

Now let's take a look and see how you can increase your potential income. Teacher salaries are based upon years of service and graduate credits earned beyond your undergraduate degree. With this in mind, when you examine a school district's pay scale, notice the salary scale, which probably resembles the following: bachelor's degree, bachelor's +15, master's, master's +30, master's +60 and a list of years ranging from 1-35. It becomes easy to see the differences in salaries as your eyes move across the page.

Here's an example of what I'm saying. Most graduate credit advances produce about $500-$3000 of increased income per year over 30 years. That means that an average increase of $2000 over those 30 years would equal about $60,000. If you factor in a good tax-deferred investment plan, this amount could easily double or triple.

Most school districts will pay for a portion, if not all, of a master's degree. Some districts will even pay for a second master's program.

It's important to note here that you will be better off over the long haul by taking graduate credits from a university and applying these credits to a degree, rather than simply taking in-service courses. Most states will give graduate credit for inservice work, but these credits will not transfer to another state. Also, it never hurts to have additional letters next to your name. How can this be accomplished? The secret is to compartmentalize your working day and your life. Utilize every working moment and find some extra time every week at home.

Another area to be aware of is your annual tax bill. Teachers not only can have a Tax Deferred Annuity (TDA) but also can deduct foreign and domestic travel, depending upon the subjects taught and your destination. Therefore, it never hurts to have your taxes prepared by a tax professional or a CPA.

 **TEACH SEZ:**

The bottom line here is simply this: If a married couple, both with master's degrees, contribute the maximum percentage of their combined salaries into a TDA investment plan over an entire career, both people can retire with a comfortable lifestyle. Plus, from day 1 to year 30, their lives can be one of self-fulfillment, travel and a lot of time off to pursue interests, hobbies and friendships!

Retirement

Speaking of retirement ... before selecting the teaching profession from the overwhelming number of offers coming your way, consider the state's retirement package for teachers along with the local school district's benefit package. These will vary, with some being better than others. Also, examine the current and projected salary scales for beginning and senior level teachers. This will reveal the district's attitudes toward senior teachers as well as the amount of pay increases each year.

In many cases, school districts grudgingly give out salary raises to senior people because of the large amount of money needed to fund that item. The school districts would prefer to put their financial resources towards a new person until the young teacher is totally dependent financially (5-7 years). Be sure, therefore, that you have an upward mobility in your salary scale for your 30-year tour.

Eventually you will want to stop working and live off your retirement earnings. As soon as possible, begin a tax-deferred annuity program. (See Appendix, page 105.) These contributions not only reduce your taxable gross income, but also grow tax-free dollars, providing you make consistent and increasing contributions over your 30-year career. Be sure to make direct entries into a variety of mutual funds and do not use an insurance company. The returns are not as great. This is the secret to retiring a millionaire. Remember, the state is not your friend. As in any negotiation, watch out for yourself!

Now let's look at what the benefit packages should minimally contain. **Remember, you are a sought-after commodity.**

Below is a list of items to negotiate or at least be aware of prior to the interview.

- State Pension (contributory/non-contributory)
- County Pension
- Blue Cross/Shield (individual vs. family costs)
- Vision and Dental
- Prescription Allowance
- Signing Bonuses (optimal)
- Percentage of pay raises/steps
- Relocation allowance

Unions

Another area worth investigating concerns the joining of a local teacher's union. Local unions can give you support and options that you wouldn't normally have. Unfortunately state and national unions have become political entities supporting candidates who often further their political objectives. The advantages of unions kick in after tenure.

PROS	CONS
Liability Insurance (a "must have")	Dollar Costs
Grievance Procedures	Political Involvement
Organizations	
Special Buying Offers	
Collective Bargaining	
State & National Representation (whatever that means)	

There are alternatives. There are a number of national unions to choose from now and private companies that offer liability insurance, at a fraction of the cost of a union package.

1. American Federation of Teachers
   AFT, 555 New Jersey Ave, NW
   Washington, DC 20001
   www.aft.org (This site has up-to-date info on national salaries.)

2. National Education Association
   1201 16th St., NW
   Washington, DC 20036
   www.nea.org

3. Association of American Educators
   26012 Marguerite Pkwy., #333
   Mission Viejo, CA 92692
   www.aaeteachers.org

SWARMING GNATS:

Books Left in the Desk:

Many students prefer to leave books in their desk rather than carry them or put them in their locker. Watch for this!

Vested Funds

One thing you should be familiar with is the idea of "vested funds." As a young teacher, it may be enjoyable to move from place to place, school to school. But a problem may develop later in your career: "lost work years." What this means is you could work for 4 years here and 6 years there and not receive credit for them in a retirement plan.

Even though you have taught for 10 years, you might lose teaching years because of hiring regulations. Some schools will only permit up to 5 years to transfer into their system; so, even if you've worked 10 years, you may find yourself on step five after being hired. That turns into lost income for each year you work in that system.

And as far as retirement goes, you may lose time, even having to work an extra 10 years to make up for the lost investment within a system's retirement plan.

The best way to counter this situation is to keep your dollar contribution invested in the state retirement plan. This is called "being vested." This means the state you worked for must contribute to your future retirement after a certain number of years of service. It's not much, but it's something you've earned. Refer to the Appendix, pages 105 and 106 for additional information on Tax Deferred Annuities (TDA).

The Bottom Line:

1. More college credits mean more dollars in your wallet; keep taking courses.

2. Set up a tax-deferred annuity.

3. Learn what you can write off on your taxes.

4. Set up a financial plan early in your career! Don't wait.

5. Get insurance to cover any potential lawsuits.

6. Mutual funds are your friend; get to know them.

7. Think carefully about your retirement plan before switching to another school system.

16: Pros & Cons

Most people don't go into teaching for the money. But frankly, the money's not bad. Some counties are paying mid to high 30s for first-year teachers. Those salaries jump into the 40s and 50s within about 7 to 10 years. Add to that about 3 months off a year (including winter break). And public schools offer excellent benefits packages. As for job security, after tenure, it's solid. So on the financial end of things, teaching is doing fine. Sure, there are those who will constantly bellyache about the pay. Avoid them. You have other more important things to focus on. Some people wouldn't know what to do if they didn't have something to complain about.

Now on the meaningful side of life, teaching has the potential to score high. You have the opportunity to mold young minds to a degree. **Impacting young lives is a noble pursuit.** Don't underestimate the honor of standing before young minds. It's a blessing. Mentor them! There's a dearth of role models in our society. Students are hungry for someone they can look up to—whether they admit it or not. Many people go into teaching because they want to have a meaningful life.

How about the cons of teaching? The work hours during the school year can be quite long and "all-consuming." The large amount of time it takes to plan and grade student work cannot be underestimated, particularly for a beginning teacher. **Try not to resent the huge number of hours you work the first year;** those hours will diminish after a couple years.

Impacting young lives is a noble pursuit.

Teaching is like working two jobs. First, you work at the school building—managing and teaching young people. The second job is what you do at home—unless you want to stay late at school. At home, you'll plan and grade a lot. You'll often find yourself trying to stay one step ahead of your students during the first year. It really is a marathon.

Other cons include some lack of autonomy, particularly with state-mandated tests. Those tests may demoralize you at times, especially if you're philosophically opposed to their content and "importance" to a young person's life. Nationwide, there's an outcry for more accountability in education. And for most, that means tests and more tests. Find out what tests are required in your state before you begin teaching.

SWARMING GNATS

Personal Leave:

This is a form of leave to be used for meetings and other personal activities you might attend during the academic year.

At the high school level particularly, the teaching profession can be rather isolating. As I often said, "I don't work with other adults. I work with students all day, then have a small chat with a colleague on the way up to the office after school, then head home."

I did make a point early on of befriending one colleague. His feedback helped keep me grounded on particularly frustrating teaching days. And, believe me, you'll have days where you really want to quit during the first year of teaching.

Promise yourself you'll teach a second year when you begin your career.

The first year can be just plain wacky: you're bombarded with so much new information, students and those administrative minutia—"swarming gnats." Hang in there!

Just remember that your school is a family system. Every system, no matter what profession you enter, has a degree of dysfunction. It's up to you to determine where your school falls on this continuum. Then you choose where you want to teach. Some counties may be much more liberal than others. And, as we've said, a principal makes a big difference to the atmosphere of a school. Many high schools get new principals about every 5 years. The old saying, "This too shall pass," really applies to a school's atmosphere.

TEACH SEZ:

One other piece of advice: avoid teachers who are just hanging on to retire. Teaching is hard enough without absorbing others' negative attitudes and/or perceptions. Don't weigh yourself down with that stuff.

In a nutshell: the pros are job security, benefits, vacation time, meaningful work. The cons are lack of autonomy, long hours, negative attitudes.

The Bottom Line:

1. June, July, August.
2. Great benefits package.
3. Hard, often all-consuming, work during school year.
4. Work to overcome negative attitudes.
5. Precise beginning and ending to each work year unlike private enterprise.
6. Remember your work is meaningful—it's not in vain!

17: Fried or Burned Out

Because of the very nature of the job and the people involved, you can expect to feel fried or burned out at least once during your first year and most years after. Teachers by their very nature are givers, while students by their very nature are takers. This, together with the normal stress of everyday living and obligations of family and friends, can leave you emotionally stretched, unless you are prepared for it!

To begin with, you must understand that we are talking here about two separate things. The hardest part of the school year will be from January to April. During this 4-month period, everyone's nerves will tighten and fatigue will set it. You are "fried." This is normal and just part of the job. Your emotions will go up and down as each new morning brings on the same routine, until the spring break. **Relief! After the break, you will find that you have caught your second wind and the last 2 to 3 months will just fly by.**

When we speak of burnout, we are talking about the many negative things that will add up over the many years. The many small daily hurts or insults, the disappointments, confrontations and administration lunacy all take their toll because your personal beliefs are put on the line and challenged every day.

The way to survive and go the distance is to compartmentalize your life and not get too emotionally involved. It is important to care, and students can easily identify those teachers who do not. But remember one thing, **do not take your work problems home with you.** You must always reserve some down time for yourself, family and friends without feeling guilty.

When you begin to take everything personally, it is only a matter of time before the unavoidable occurs — burnout! This usually happens around the 7th or 8th year. Don't confuse your personal emotional baggage with the stress of the job.

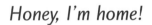

Honey, I'm home!

Looking back over the past 30 years, the biggest reason I've seen for the burnout phenomenon seems to be the daily conflict between one's beliefs and the bureaucratic chores. As an example, let's suppose you fail a student who rightfully deserves the failing grade. This student has attempted to create disturbances and problems, has refused to do classwork and has worked to undermine your classroom authority. As a result, the grade would appear to be just. Correct? Wrong!

How are you going to feel when word comes down that you cannot fail this child because of his/her 504 plan or you forgot to call the parent who now is very upset? These little defeats will eventually eat you up!

TEACH SEZ: **The solution is to stay emotionally detached and flexible, much like your doctor or lawyer; and work closely, efficiently and effectively with the students while maintaining an emotionally healthy distance.**

The Bottom Line:

1. Don't take things personally.
2. Compartmentalize your life.
3. Use mental health days when needed.
4. Use group activity days in the classroom once a week.
5. Relax and go with the flow!
6. Remember that everyone is feeling what you are feeling. It's just part of the 10-month cycle.

18: Going the Distance

Effective teachers are enthusiastic about what they do each day. They clearly find their subject matter worthwhile and even show some passion about it now and then. Cultivate a love of your material. If you don't care about what you're teaching, why would you expect the students to care about it?

If you're bored with your material, then the students will be bored too. As a teacher, it is within your power to alter how you teach in your classroom. You will also have many opportunities to supplement the required curriculum with your favorite material or pet research topic.

I always do my best to "teach from where I'm at." That has helped me to maintain some enthusiasm. If I read a great article in the Sunday paper, I'll clip it, copy it and distribute it on Monday or Tuesday for discussion. If I suddenly find orangutans fascinating, I'll steer the curriculum in such a way as to incorporate the furry orange creatures. If I see a powerful or moving film, I'll show a clip from it as a writing prompt or discussion starter. **As a teacher you've got to keep yourself fresh.** If you simply do the same thing over and over and over and over, you will become extremely bored and so will your students.

So teach from where you're at, what grabs and inspires you. A creative teacher can find ways to incorporate just about anything into a curriculum, and with a solid rationale! If you're feeling discouraged or noncreative, find a teacher to talk to. Hey, you're a first-year teacher; veteran teachers will expect you to be asking questions! And some may even enjoy the fact that a new teacher is asking them to share what they know.

Try to observe the teachers with strong reputations. It doesn't matter if they teach a different discipline. Just watch their techniques, how they engage students in the subject matter. You can learn a lot just from observing a master teacher. Don't be embarrassed to ask permission to observe another teacher!

By getting in the "Enthusiasm Habit" right from the get-go, you will be well on your way to GOING THE DISTANCE. In order to complete your tour of 30 years and reap the benefits you so richly deserve, we have concluded that the following characteristics are crucial to that goal.

What It Takes to Go the Distance

1. You must be able to be flexible and adaptable to changing situations.

2. You must develop a good sense of humor.

3. You must perfect a style of organization management which utilizes every minute of the working day to allow "down time" at home.

4. You must plan alternatives to the original game plan.

5. You must learn to interact and create bridges with other personalities.

6. Remain loyal to your "core of beliefs."

7. Remain loyal to the "chair of the principalship."

8. Remember your position as the "Benevolent Dictator."

9. Always keep and maintain control.

10. Learn to pick the battles that you can win.

11. Read and learn your contract.

12. Keep and maintain friends and interests outside of the school and the profession (most important).

13. Be able to do more than one thing at a time.

14. Always stick by your word.

The Bottom Line:

1. Teach from your heart.

2. If you're bored, the students probably are too!

3. It's within your power to make things interesting for you and them.

4. Surround yourself with positive people.

5. Maintain a hobby.

Appendices

Appendix A:
Bill Gates Speaks

Here's some advice Bill Gates recently dished out at a high school speech about 11 things they don't teach in school. He talks about how "feel-good," politically correct teaching has created a full generation of kids with no concept of reality and how this lack of knowledge has set them up for failure in the real world.

RULE #1: Life is not fair—get used to it.

RULE #2: The world won't care about your self-esteem. The world will expect you to accomplish something before you feel good about yourself.

RULE #3: You will NOT make $40,000 a year right out of high school. You won't be a vice president with a car phone, until you earn both.

RULE #4: If you think your teacher is tough, wait till you get a boss. He doesn't have tenure.

RULE #5: Flipping burgers is not beneath your dignity. Your grandparents had a word for burger flipping—they called it opportunity.

RULE #6: If you mess up, it's not your parent's fault, so don't whine about your mistakes; learn from them.

RULE #7: Before you were born, your parents weren't as boring as they are now. They got that way from paying your bills, cleaning your clothes and listening to you talk about how cool you are. So, before you save the rain forest from the parasites of your parents' generation, try delousing the closet in your own room.

RULE #8: Your school may have done away with winners and losers, but life has not. In some schools they have abolished failing grades, and they'll give you as many times as you want to get the right answer. This doesn't bear the slightest resemblance to ANYTHING in real life.

RULE #9: Life is not divided into semesters. You don't get summers and Christmas breaks off, and very few employers are interested in helping you find yourself. Do that on your own time.

RULE #10: Television is NOT real life. In real life people actually have to leave the coffee shop and report to jobs.

RULE #11: Be nice to nerds. Chances are you'll end up working for one.

Point Sheet Sample

DATE	ASSIGNMENT	POINTS POSSIBLE	POINTS ACHIEVED

Notice of Detention

Date _____   Grade _____

As a disciplinary measure, I have found it necessary to detain your child after school. It is important that you, the parent, read this notice and help to change the negative behavior before it requires a more serious disciplinary action.

A student who fails to return his/her detention form or who fails to keep the appointment may be referred to the administration for possible suspension. A parent conference would then be necessary before said student would be readmitted to school.

_____ is required to stay after school from _____ To _____
           (Student)   (Time)   (Time)

on _____ for the following reason(s):
    (Date)

_____ Disrespect   _____ Failure to Follow a   _____ Lateness to Class
                                                          Reasonable Request

_____ Disruption   _____ Not Participating in
                                             _____ Unprepared for Class   Class Activities

_____ Destruction of
         Property   _____ Violation of School/   _____ Cutting Class
                                                         Class Rules
_____ Inciting Others   _____ Insubordination

_____ Other: _____

_____

Comments: _____

If a student must miss his/her assigned detention due to illness or a family emergency, a parent may telephone the school between the hours of _____ and _____ to arrange for an alternate detention date.

Please make arrangements for transporting your child at the appropriate time after the detention period. Your child is required to return this letter, signed by you.

_____
                                            Instructor

I understand that my child has been assigned a detention for violating school and/or classroom rules and I accept the responsibility for providing transportation for him/her on the above date(s).

_____
                                       Parent/Guardian

Referral Sample

_____ - Administrator

Student's Name _____ Date _____

Teacher _____ Grade _____ Period _____

Subject _____ Present Grade in Subject _____

Reason for Referral (be specific as to offense): _____

_____

_____

_____

_____

The primary responsibility for pupil conduct rests with the classroom teacher. The Administration will give all reasonable support in the fulfillment of this responsibility.

Steps taken by teacher before this referral:

_____ Teacher Counseling   _____ Phone Call to Parent

_____ Punishment Assignment/Detention   _____ Parent/Teacher Conference

_____ Guidance Referral   _____ Counselor/Teacher Conference

_____ Admin./Teacher Conference   _____ _____
                                                        (Other)

Administrative Action: _____

_____

_____

_____

_____

_____
Administrator

Rating Observation Form

Name: _____ Date: _____ Time: _____ to _____

School: _____ Subject & Grade: _____

Overall rating of this lesson: ☐ Satisfactory ☐ Needs Improvement

SKILL	NA	S	NI
1. Chooses appropriate content.	☐	☐	☐
2. Presents content in a way that demonstrates mastery of subject	☐	☐	☐
3. Paces instruction appropriately.	☐	☐	☐
4. Creates desirable learning environment	☐	☐	☐
5. Communicates realistically high expectations	☐	☐	☐
6. Uses instructional time efficiently	☐	☐	☐
7. Keeps students on task	☐	☐	☐
8. Provides organizing structure	☐	☐	☐
9. Uses appropriate strategies and activities	☐	☐	☐
10. Ensures active participation	☐	☐	☐
11. Monitors student learning	☐	☐	☐
12. Questions effectively	☐	☐	☐
13. Responds effectively	☐	☐	☐

SUPPORTING SKILLS

	NA	S	NI
1. Allocates instructional time to reflect curricular priorities, makes appropriate plans	☐	☐	☐
2. Uses tests consistent with instructional objectives	☐	☐	☐
3. Grades student learning fairly, objectively, validly	☐	☐	☐
4. Provides instruction related to specified curricular goals	☐	☐	☐

OBSERVATIONS/RECOMMENDATIONS

SPECIAL STRENGTHS OBSERVED: SKILLS USED WITH HIGH DEGREE OF EFFECTIVENESS

RECOMMENDATIONS FOR IMPROVEMENT

TEACHER COMMENTS

Signature of Observer(s):   Signature of Teacher:

_____   _____

_____

Date of Conference: _____

Summative Evaluation Form

TEACHER'S NAME: _____ SCHOOL YEAR: _____ _____

SCHOOL: _____ ASSIGNMENT: _____

| SPECIFIC RATINGS: Observable instructional skills *(Teaching Efficiency/Scholarship)* Rate teacher's overall performance for the year. | | SPECIFIC RATINGS: Non-observable instructional skills. Rate teacher's overall performance for the year. | |

Observable instructional skills (Teaching Efficiency/Scholarship)

	S	U
1. Chooses appropriate content	☐	☐
2. Presents content in a way that demonstrates mastery of subject matter	☐	☐
3. Paces instruction appropriately	☐	☐
4. Creates desirable learning environment	☐	☐
5. Communicates realistically high expectations . . .	☐	☐
6. Uses instructional time efficiently	☐	☐
7. Keeps students on task	☐	☐
8. Provides organizing structure	☐	☐
9. Uses appropriate strategies, activities	☐	☐
10. Ensures active participation	☐	☐
11. Monitors student learning	☐	☐
12. Questions effectively	☐	☐
13. Responds effectively	☐	☐

SPECIFIC RATINGS: Non-observable instructional skills.
Rate teacher's overall performance for the year.

	S	U
1. Allocates instructional time in a manner that reflects curricular priorities and makes appropriate plans	☐	☐
2. Uses tests consistent with objectives	☐	☐
3. Grades fairly, objectively, validly	☐	☐
4. Provides instruction related to specified curricular goals	☐	☐

SPECIFIC RATINGS: Administrative Duties.
Rate teacher's overall performance for the year.

	S	U
1. Keeps records and reports accurately, neatly, properly	☐	☐
2. Follows federal, state, and local policies and procedures	☐	☐
3. Is regular in attendance and is punctual	☐	☐
4. Communicates effectively with parents	☐	☐

SUPPORTING DATA

EVALUATOR'S COMMENTS:

TEACHER'S COMMENTS:

*EMPLOYEE SIGNATURE:

_____

CONFERENCE DATE: _____

OVERALL RATING: ☐ SATISFACTORY
                    ☐ UNSATISFACTORY

RECOMMEND:
  ☐ RE-EMPLOY   ☐ DISMISSAL
  ☐ NON-RENEWAL ☐ SECOND CLASS

PRINCIPAL/EVALUATOR(S) SIGNATURE:

_____ DATE: _____

_____ DATE: _____

Contribution Comparison

	Paycheck Before Joining Plan	Paycheck After Joining Plan
Income After Adjustments	$1,154	$1,154
Tax-Deferred Contribution	-0	-75
Net Taxable Income	1,154	1,079
Federal Income Tax (28%)	-323	-302
Take Home Pay	$ 831	$ 777

Tax Deferred Annuity Contribution Sample

Assuming 8-1/2% Return and 26 Pay Periods

	After-Tax Savings Plan	Tax-Deferred Annuity
Bi-weekly contribution	$ 75	$ 75
Less income tax (28%)	-21	-0
Net bi-weekly contribution	54	75
Net yearly contribution	$ 1,404	$ 1,950
After 10 Years		
Total contribution	$ 14,040	$ 19,500
Investment earnings at 8.5%	+7,161	+10,689
Less income tax on earnings (28%)	-2,005	-0
Total	$ 19,196	$ 30,189
After 20 Years		
Total contribution	$ 28,080	$ 39,000
Investment earnings at 8.5%	+35,951	+59,444
Less income tax on earnings (28%)	-10,066	-0
Total	$ 53,965	$ 98,444
After 30 Years		
Total contribution	$ 42,120	$ 58,500
Investment earnings at 8.5%	+103,915	+194,269
Less income tax on earnings (28%)	-29,096	-0
Total	$116,939	$252,769

PERSONAL JOURNAL

YEAR ONE

The purpose of this journal is to help you establish "working guidelines" for next year. Please answer these questions at the end of each of the related time periods. Don't be afraid to go back and compare your responses as the year progresses.

First Day

What was your biggest surprise?

What expectations did not occur?

What expectations did occur?

What were your greatest concerns or fears?

How do you feel?

List the problems you confronted.

List the successes you achieved.

What would you have done differently?

PERSONAL JOURNAL

First Week

What was your biggest surprise?

What expectations did not occur?

What expectations did occur?

What were your greatest concerns or fears?

How do you feel?

List the problems you confronted.

List the successes you achieved.

What would you have done differently?

Second Week

What was your biggest surprise?

What expectations did not occur?

What expectations did occur?

What were your greatest concerns or fears?

How do you feel?

List the problems you confronted.

List the successes you achieved.

What would you have done differently?

Third Week

What was your biggest surprise? _____

_____

What expectations did not occur? _____

_____

What expectations did occur? _____

_____

_____

_____

What were your greatest concerns or fears? _____

_____

_____

_____

How do you feel? _____

_____

_____

List the problems you confronted. _____

_____

_____

_____

List the successes you achieved. _____

_____

_____

_____

What would you have done differently? _____

_____

_____

_____

Fourth Week

What was your biggest surprise?

What expectations did not occur?

What expectations did occur?

What were your greatest concerns or fears?

How do you feel?

List the problems you confronted.

List the successes you achieved.

What would you have done differently?

PERSONAL JOURNAL

Fifth Week

What was your biggest surprise? _____
_____

What expectations did not occur? _____
_____

What expectations did occur? _____
_____
_____
_____

What were your greatest concerns or fears? _____
_____
_____
_____

How do you feel? _____
_____
_____

List the problems you confronted. _____
_____
_____
_____

List the successes you achieved. _____
_____
_____
_____

What would you have done differently? _____
_____
_____
_____

Sixth Week

What was your biggest surprise?

What expectations did not occur?

What expectations did occur?

What were your greatest concerns or fears?

How do you feel?

List the problems you confronted.

List the successes you achieved.

What would you have done differently?

First Marking Period

What was your biggest surprise?

What expectations did not occur?

What expectations did occur?

What were your greatest concerns or fears?

How do you feel?

List the problems you confronted.

List the successes you achieved.

What would you have done differently?

Second Marking Period

What was your biggest surprise?

What expectations did not occur?

What expectations did occur?

What were your greatest concerns or fears?

How do you feel?

List the problems you confronted.

List the successes you achieved.

What would you have done differently?

PERSONAL JOURNAL

Third Marking Period

What was your biggest surprise?

What expectations did not occur?

What expectations did occur?

What were your greatest concerns or fears?

How do you feel?

List the problems you confronted.

List the successes you achieved.

What would you have done differently?

Fourth Marking Period

What was your biggest surprise?

What expectations did not occur?

What expectations did occur?

What were your greatest concerns or fears?

How do you feel?

List the problems you confronted.

List the successes you achieved.

What would you have done differently?

PERSONAL JOURNAL

Final Exam

What was your biggest surprise? _____

_____

What expectations did not occur? _____

_____

What expectations did occur? _____

_____

_____

What were your greatest concerns or fears? _____

_____

_____

_____

How do you feel? _____

_____

_____

List the problems you confronted. _____

_____

_____

_____

List the successes you achieved. _____

_____

_____

_____

What would you have done differently? _____

_____

_____

TRENCH TEACHING

Proven Tactics for the High School Teacher

☐ I am enclosing my check. ☐ You may email me for credit card information.

☐ I am interested in discounted multiple quantity pricing.

☐ I am interested in more information about workshops presented by **THE TRENCH TEACHING CONSORTIUM**.

☐ Please add me to your email list for future releases.

☐ Other _____

Name _____
    PLEASE PRINT CLEARLY FOR ACCURATE SHIPPING INFO!

Address _____

City _____ State _____ Zip _____

Email _____

The Trench Teaching Consortium, PO Box 215, Owings, MD 20736

___ copies @ $17.50   = $_____

TAX (5% MD ONLY)   = $_____

SUBTOTAL   = $_____

___ S&H @ $4.00   = $_____

TOTAL ENCLOSED   = $_____

If you desire to pay by check, please make it payable to The Trench Teaching Consortium and enclose with this card in an envelope. To pay by credit card, you may visit www.trenchteaching.com or check the box above to be emailed for credit card information.

TRENCH TEACHING

Proven Tactics for the High School Teacher

VISIT OUR WEBSITE:
www.trenchteaching.com

☐ I am enclosing my check. ☐ You may email me for credit card information.

☐ I am interested in discounted multiple quantity pricing.

☐ I am interested in more information about workshops presented by **THE TRENCH TEACHING CONSORTIUM**.

☐ Please add me to your email list for future releases.

☐ Other _____

Name _____
    PLEASE PRINT CLEARLY FOR ACCURATE SHIPPING INFO!

Address _____

City _____ State _____ Zip _____

Email _____

The Trench Teaching Consortium, PO Box 215, Owings, MD 20736

___ copies @ $17.50   = $_____

TAX (5% MD ONLY)   = $_____

SUBTOTAL   = $_____

___ S&H @ $4.00   = $_____

TOTAL ENCLOSED   = $_____

If you desire to pay by check, please make it payable to The Trench Teaching Consortium and enclose with this card in an envelope. To pay by credit card, you may visit www.trenchteaching.com or check the box above to be emailed for credit card information.

TRENCH TEACHING

TRENCH TEACHING

TRENCH TEACHING

VISIT OUR WEBSITE:
www.trenchteaching.com

Proven Tactics for the High School Teacher

❑ I am enclosing my check. ❑ You may email me for credit card information.

❑ I am interested in discounted multiple quantity pricing.

❑ I am interested in more information about workshops presented by **THE TRENCH TEACHING CONSORTIUM**.

❑ Please add me to your email list for future releases.

❑ Other _____

Name _____
PLEASE PRINT CLEARLY FOR ACCURATE SHIPPING INFO!

Address _____

City _____ State _____ Zip _____

Email _____

The Trench Teaching Consortium, PO Box 215, Owings, MD 20736

___ copies @ $17.50 = $_____

TAX (5% MD ONLY) = $_____

SUBTOTAL = $_____

___ S&H @ $4.00 = $_____

TOTAL ENCLOSED = $_____

If you desire to pay by check, please make it payable to The Trench Teaching Consortium and enclose with this card in an envelope. To pay by credit card, you may visit www.trenchteaching.com or check the box above to be emailed for credit card information.

TRENCH TEACHING

VISIT OUR WEBSITE:
www.trenchteaching.com

Proven Tactics for the High School Teacher

❑ I am enclosing my check. ❑ You may email me for credit card information.

❑ I am interested in discounted multiple quantity pricing.

❑ I am interested in more information about workshops presented by **THE TRENCH TEACHING CONSORTIUM**.

❑ Please add me to your email list for future releases.

❑ Other _____

Name _____
PLEASE PRINT CLEARLY FOR ACCURATE SHIPPING INFO!

Address _____

City _____ State _____ Zip _____

Email _____

The Trench Teaching Consortium, PO Box 215, Owings, MD 20736

___ copies @ $17.50 = $_____

TAX (5% MD ONLY) = $_____

SUBTOTAL = $_____

___ S&H @ $4.00 = $_____

TOTAL ENCLOSED = $_____

If you desire to pay by check, please make it payable to The Trench Teaching Consortium and enclose with this card in an envelope. To pay by credit card, you may visit www.trenchteaching.com or check the box above to be emailed for credit card information.

TRENCH TEACHING

TRENCH TEACHING